NARRATIVE
OF THE
FAMINE IN INDIA
1896-97

NARRATIVE

OF THE

FAMINE IN INDIA

1896-97

T. W. HOLDERNESS

GYAN

Published by

Gyan Publishing House
5, Ansari Road
Daryaganj, New Delhi-110002
Phone: 011-47034999, 9811692060
E-mail: books@gyanbooks.com

Distribution Network
gyanbooks.com
India, USA, Canada, UK, Australia

ISBN: 978-93-7014-230-5 (HB)

First Published, 1897

2nd Impression 2025

Printed at: Gyan Press, Delhi.

NARRATIVE OF THE FAMINE IN INDIA 1896-97
Author: T. W. HOLDERNESS

NARRATIVE

OF THE

FAMINE IN INDIA

IN

1896-97.

BY

T. W. HOLDERNESS, I.C.S.,

DEPUTY SECRETARY (FAMINE) TO THE GOVERNMENT OF INDIA.

1897.

CONTENTS.

APPENDICES.

NARRATIVE OF THE FAMINE OF 1896–97.

1. The account given in these pages of the famine of 1896-97 has no claim to be more than an imperfect sketch put together from incomplete and scattered materials. For a complete review of the subject the reports of the Provincial Governments are required, and some time must elapse before all of these are ready. Famine operations have nearly closed in Bengal, the North-Western Provinces and the Punjab. But in the Central Provinces the relief of distress still occupies the energies of the local administration, notwithstanding that agricultural prospects there are excellent ; while in Madras, Bombay, and Burma the protraction of the period of drought till the end of August makes it at present difficult to say when relief operations there will completely terminate. It is thought that a general account of the famine will be of some interest while its events are still fresh, and that a detailed discussion of the measures undertaken to combat it and of the questions of administrative policy which arose from time to time during the progress of these measures may be postponed until more complete information is available.

I.—The cause of the famine.

2. The cause of the famine of 1897 was the early cessation of the autumn rains of 1896. The south-west monsoon was late in establishing itself in June 1896 on the West Coast, and from its first appearance was ill-distributed and fitful in character. Throughout July the rainfall was more or less deficient in Bengal and Central and Northern India, and gave rise to apprehensions. In August the monsoon appeared to have recovered strength, and frequent cyclonic storms gave heavy rain to the Central Provinces, Central India, and Rajputana. Elsewhere in Upper India the rainfall was in defect. Early in September the hopes of an improving monsoon were disappointed. The rainfall was in large defect over by far the greatest part of India, and was in excess only in East and North Bengal, South India, and Lower Burma. During this month irretrievable injury was sustained by the rain crops. In the North-Western Provinces and Oudh the average rainfall in September is from 5 to 8 inches, being lowest in the west and highest in the east. In September 1896 no division of the provinces received more than 1 inch, and in most the fall was considerably less. In the Punjab the fall was under half an inch, except in the north and the hill divisions, against an average of 3 to 5 inches. In the Central Provinces less than half an inch fell in the western and central tracks where the average September rainfall exceeds eight inches. Berar received ·38 of an inch against an average of 6·23 inches. The fall in Rajputana and Central India was equally small. In the Bombay Deccan 1·20 inches fell against an average of 5·53 inches, and in Khandesh ·96 of an inch against 7 inches. In the Madras Deccan the fall varied from 1 to 2 inches against an average of 5 inches. In Bengal and Behar the defect was less, and but for the cessation of the south-west monsoon early in the following month this part of India would have escaped without serious damage. In October virtually no rain fell in the Punjab, the North-Western Provinces and Oudh, Rajputana, Central India, the Central Provinces, or Berar. In the Bombay and Madras Deccan from $\frac{1}{4}$ to 1 inch fell in place of the normal rainfall of 4 to 6 inches. This following the protracted drought of September completed the ruin of the crops over vast areas, and made sowings for the cold weather crops almost impossible without the help of irrigation. In Bengal the October rainfall is in ordinary years larger in amount and of even more importance, on account of the late rice crop, than in Upper India. In most divisions in Bengal proper the average fall in October is from 4 to 6 inches: and in Behar nearly 3 inches. In October 1896 Behar was rainless, and throughout Bengal proper the fall in most divisions was under 1 inch. Orissa received ·09 of an inch against an average of 5·85. The late or winter rice crop, representing half the total cropped area of the Province, sustained great injury. In many places three-quarters of the crop was lost. For the whole of Bengal, Orissa and Behar

the yield of the rice crop is returned at 9½ million tons against 20½ millions, a loss of more than half the crop.

The early withdrawal of a weak south-west monsoon was followed by a still weaker north-east monsoon, on which the eastern and central districts of Madras chiefly depend. In the central districts only ·36 of an inch fell in October against an average of 5·21 inches; and along the East Coast the deficiency was still greater.

3. Thus the month of October closed with the entire Indian continent face to face with the most wide-spread failure of the rains and the gravest impending famine of the century. From this extreme peril it was rescued by most opportune and unlooked for rain in the succeeding month.

4. In the first week of November scattered showers fell in the Punjab and Southern India, which were followed by continuous heavy rain over the central and southern divisions of Madras. In the middle of the month there was good rain in the Bombay Presidency, and this extended to the Central Provinces, Berar, Mysore, Hyderabad, the North-Western Provinces and Oudh, Central India and Rajputana, Behar and Bengal. Outside the Madras Presidency and the Bombay Deccan the amount of rain registered in most tracts was under 1 inch, but it enabled cold weather crops to be very largely sown on unirrigated lands with fair hope of the seed germinating. In the Bombay Deccan considerably over 1 inch of rain fell, in Mysore over 2½ inches. Thus the effect of the November rain was to confine serious crop-failure in the Bombay and Madras Presidencies to the relatively small and sparsely populated area of the Deccan districts, and to secure a cold weather crop in Central and Upper India—scanty in extent, it is true, and sown under unfavourable conditions, but still sufficient to very materially supplement the depleted stocks of the country. From November the scarcity, though serious, shrank within measurable dimensions.

5. The month of December was as abnormally wet as November. Fairly general rain in moderate amounts, aggregating about 1 inch or less, was recorded during the month in most provinces, enabling sowings to be carried on to the end of the year and greatly benefiting the crops already sown. In the Deccan country and in the Nizam's Dominions the falls were very slight, and in this part of India the crops sown after the November rain as a rule absolutely failed. But elsewhere the month closed with better prospects for the sown lands than were thought possible in October.

6. These prospects were maintained by light to moderate rain in many parts of Upper and Central India during January and February. In the latter part of February and the beginning of March hot winds did a good deal of damage to the crops on unirrigated lands, and anxiety was felt lest they should be completely dried up before maturity. But in the middle of March the approach of the hot weather was arrested by frequent storms. Rain fell in good quantities in North Behar, Central and Upper India, greatly benefiting the ripening cold weather crops and permitting extra crops of early millet to be sown in many places. The Bombay and Madras Deccan continued rainless.

7. In April the cold weather crops were reaped in Behar, the North-Western Provinces and Oudh, the Central Provinces and the Southern Punjab, and agricultural operations throughout the greater part of India ceased for the time, and the absence or presence of rain became of little consequence. In the North Punjab, where the cold weather harvest is later, good rain fell during the month and improved the crops.

8. With April the second period of the scarcity may be said to have closed, as the first period may be said to have closed in October. With May another agricultural year opened, and another phase of the situation commenced. The month was favourable for Bengal and Lower Burma. Southerly winds from the Bay gave good rain in these parts and sowings of early rain crops commenced. But no advance of the south-west monsoon was reported in Southern India, and the first week of June passed before it appeared on the Ceylon coast. In the middle of June more favourable conditions appeared. Rain was received throughout India, and the monsoon winds blew strongly on the west coast and

across Central India. But this strength was of short duration. In the second half of the month the rainfall everywhere fell off, hot winds began to blow, and hot weather conditions seemed to be re-established. This period of great anxiety lasted into July. In the first week of July a marked improvement occurred, and by the middle of the month ordinary monsoon conditions were established in Upper India, though the rainfall was light and the Bombay and Madras Deccan received only scattered showers. At the end of the month conditions still further improved, and during August heavy continuous rain fell in Bengal, the Central Provinces, the North Western Provinces and Oudh, the west coast districts of Bombay, Rajputana and Central India, extending in the middle of the month to the Punjab.

9. September opened with excellent agricultural prospects in every part of India excepting in the "dry zone" districts of Upper Burma, the Deccan districts of Madras and Bombay, and portions of the Nizam's dominions. During the first fortnight of the month good rain fell in these excepted areas and agricultural prospects greatly improved. Such of the early sown rain crops as had escaped the drought revived, and sowings for the later crop have been vigorously prosecuted. Over much of the Deccan, specially in the heavy "black soil" tracts a very large area is not sown even in ordinary years until the heavy rains of August and September. There is thus still time for the Deccan by means of a late harvest to retrieve its fortunes, though the return to lower prices and abundant food supplies will be postponed, and relief will have to be administered for a longer period than was anticipated. Elsewhere the September rains have been favourable, assuring not only the fast ripening autumn harvest but also successful sowings for the cold weather crops. The disappearance of famine is now a question merely of weeks.

II.—The areas and populations affected.

10. It is impossible to exhibit in a statistical form with any approach to accuracy the areas affected by the almost universal drought and failure of crops which occurred in 1896–97. If the extreme south of the Peninsula and Lower Burma and such exceptional tracts as the Meerut Division in the North-Western Provinces, the Chenab irrigation colonies in the Punjab, and Sindh be excluded, a bad or indifferent autumn harvest and short sowings for the cold weather crops were chronicled almost everywhere. Where the deficiency was not very great and where past harvests had been bounteous, the agricultural classes have passed through the ordeal with tolerable ease, and in exceptional cases have actually been gainers by the high prices which their surplus grain-stocks have commanded. But everywhere the stress of high prices has been felt by the urban population, by the landless farm-labourers in rural tracts, and generally by all persons in receipt of small fixed incomes. The figures given below which have been compiled from the monthly famine reports of Provincial Governments and Native States refer to those areas only in which distress was so general and pronounced as to require relief operations to be undertaken by the State. In many cases these areas comprise fractions of a "district," the ordinary unit of Indian administration. One-half of a district may have been able to weather the storm without relief works or poor houses and with only such assistance as is afforded to the agricultural classes by temporary suspensions of the land-revenue demand ; while the other half, through greater deficiency of rainfall or absence of irrigation or peculiarities of crops, has required the relief provisions of the Famine Code to be brought into effect. The division into distressed and non-distressed tracts is thus in a measure arbitrary, and the statistical result is to narrow the area affected by the drought. The distinction between severely and slightly distressed tracts is also an uncertain one, and the table below does not pretend to accuracy in this respect. It has more than once happened that a district has passed during the scarcity from the slightly affected to the severely distressed state, and back again to the former class on the harvesting of the cold weather crops. There is no clear criterion of this distinction, and more often than not the distinction is ignored in the provincial returns. In the observations which follow the table an endeavour is made to indicate, so far as the information permits, the areas in which acute or severe distress prevailed.

I.—*British India.*

Province.	Total area of districts in which distress prevailed.	Total population.	Distressed area.		
			Area.	Population.	
	Square miles.		*Square miles.*		
Madras	27,106	3,700,000	15,000	2,000,000	Also 8,000 s miles affe with popul 2,500,000.
Bombay	48,179	8,013,000	33,000	5,500,000	Also 9,000 s miles affe with popul 1,200,000.
Bengal	54,771	24,728,000	26,000	11,200,000	
North-Western Provinces and Oudh	43,348	19,586,000	35,000	14,000,000	Also 16.000 s miles affe with popu 9,000,000.
Central Provinces	87,086	10,811,000	52,000	6,500,000	
Punjab	19,857	5,366,000	13,000	3,500,000	
Burma	10,449	776,000	5,000	500,000	
Berar	15,094	2,580,000	15,000	2,500,000	
TOTAL	305,890	75,560,000	194,000	45,700,000	

II.—*Native States.*

State.	Total area of States.	Total population.	Area affected.	Population of area affected.
Hyderabad	82,698	11,537,000	9,000	1,219,000
Central India.				
Gwalior	13,024	1,944,000	4,200	771,000
Baghelkhand	14,676	1,776,000	14,500	1,778,000
Bundelkhand	9,924	1,424,000	9,900	1,428,000
Rajputana.				
Bhurtpur	1,974	639,000	1,300	440,000
Bikanir	22,340	832,000	18,750	587,000
Dholpur	1,197	291,000	1,200	291,000
Jaisalmir	16,062	116,000	16,000	115,000
Marwar	35,000	2,526,000	6,900	235,000
Tonk	1,705	286,000	750	134,000
Total	198,600	21,371,000	82,500	6,998,000
GRAND TOTAL ...	504,490	96,931,000	276,500	52,698,000

Madras.

11. In the Madras Presidency two distinct areas were affected—the Deccan, and the northern districts on the East Coast known as the Circars. In the Deccan distress was severe over approximately one-half of the Kurnool, Bellary, Anantapur and Cuddapah districts which have an area of 27,106 square miles and a population of 3,700,000. The distressed portion was described in November 1896

by the Madras Famine Commissioner as "a broad band occupying the north-western part of Cuddapah, the taluks of Kurnool immediately adjoining to the north, the northern half of Anantapur and the eastern half of Bellary with some parts of Kurnool adjoining. This tract largely consists of stiff "black cotton" soils which are not usually sown till September, and which in 1896, in consequence of the failure of the September and October rains, were either left unsown or yielded but a scanty crop. The rest of these four Deccan districts also suffered from the defective rainfall of 1896, but owing partly to the predominance of lighter soils and partly to receiving larger amounts of rain, the harvests there were better. In the Circars relief measures have been undertaken over scattered areas aggregating 8,600 square miles with a population of 3,000,000. In these tracts distress was later in declaring itself and was throughout sporadic in type, and the numbers on relief have been relatively small. Employing the terminology of the Famine Commission the distress in the Deccan has been classed as severe and in the Circars as slight.

Bombay.

12. The whole of the Bombay Presidency (excluding Sind) suffered from the premature cessation of the south-west monsoon of 1896, and everywhere a bad or indifferent autumn harvest and short sowings of the cold weather crops were reported. But actual distress was confined to the belt of country lying above the western ghats and comprising the Deccan and South Mahratta districts. The area classified as severely distressed includes the whole of the Bijapur, Sholapur, Ahmednagar and Nasik districts, four-fifths of the Satara district, one-half of the Poona district, one-third of the Belgaum district, and scattered portions of the Khandesh district. The rest (9,000 square miles) of the Khandesh district is shown as slightly distressed. Of the distressed districts the most severely and generally afflicted was Bijapur. In it the autumn harvests absolutely failed over the whole district, and very little land was sown with cold weather crops. In Sholapur the crop-failure on unirrigated lands was equally complete, but in places there is a fair amount of tank and well irrigation which was utilised to the full. In Ahmednagar and Nasik the western portions suffered less than the eastern, and distress was less general and less acute than in Bijapur or Sholapur. In the portion of the Poona district classed as distressed distress was undoubtedly severe. In Satara, Belgaum and Khandesh relief has been confined within relatively small limits.

Bengal.

13. In Bengal the severely distressed area is shown as 26,000 square miles with a population of 11,200,000, but relief operations on a large scale were confined to 11,466 square miles and a population of 7,552,000 in the densely populated province of Behar. Of the remaining area 10,035 square miles with a population of 1,787,000 lay in the hilly and sparsely populated division of Chota Nagpur, the indigenous races of which were exposed to a certain amount of privation from failure of crops and high prices, but succeeded in maintaining themselves without general resort to the relief offered to them. In the Presidency Division portions of the Nuddea, Khulna, and Murshidabad districts, with an aggregate area of 1,568 square miles and a population of 849,000; in the Bhagalpur Division portions of the Bhagalpur district and of the Sonthal Parganas, with an area of 1,921 square miles and a population of 702,000; and in the Orissa Division a small tract in the Puri District, required a limited amount of relief. The effect of high prices and the great deficiency in the rice crop were felt more or less severely throughout the province, and test works were opened from time to time in several other districts. But as they failed to attract workers, the people had presumably larger resources than was imagined. No exceptional mortality, it may be remarked, occurred in Bengal. Even in Behar, in parts of which severe distress prevailed, the death-rate has been normal throughout the year.

The North-Western Provinces and Oudh.

14. In the North-Western Provinces and Oudh, the severely distressed area is shown as 35,000 square miles with a population of 14,000,000, and the slightly distressed area as 16,000 square miles with a population of 9,000,000. The only portions of the province where relief operations were not required were the Meerut Division in the west, the hill districts of the Kumaun Division, and the districts of Ghazipur and Bahraich in the East. But even in these tracts the harvests were

below the average. In two well marked areas distress was exceptionally severe. The first included the districts of Banda, Jalaun, Hamirpur, Jhansi, Allahabad (part), lying south of the Jumna, and known as the Bundelkhand districts of the Allahabad Division. This tract is geographically part of the rugged hill country of Central India. With a precarious rainfall, few facilities for irrigation, a poor and unskilful population, and indifferent methods of agriculture, these districts have often been visited by famine. They had passed through one such year when the rains of 1896 failed. Judged by the extent of crop-failure and by the complete exhaustion of the resources of the people, the recent famine equals in intensity any previous famine in this region. The second area of severe famine included central and southern Oudh, distress being exceptionally severe in the district of Hardoi. Outside these two areas there was severe distress in the Azamgarh and Gorakhpur districts in the east which border on Behar, and in the lower part of the Gangetic Doab, including part of the Agra Division. The slightly distressed area comprises Rohilkhand, parts of the Agra Division, and Northern and Eastern Oudh. Up to April there was severe distress in the whole of the Agra Division and in East Oudh, but with the harvesting of the cold weather crops the circumstances of the people there greatly improved.

Central Provinces.

15. In the Central Provinces the area returned as severely distressed represents three-fifths of the whole area of the provinces. No district of the 18 into which they are divided is absent from the return. In four districts (Nagpur, Chanda, Wardha and Sambalpur) small areas only were affected; in four others (Raipur, Chhindwara, Bhandara, Balaghat) the affected area varied from one-third to a half of the district. In the remaining 10 districts the whole area was distressed. Taking the Provinces with reference to their geographical divisions, it will be seen that no part has altogether escaped the drought and its consequences. In the Vindhyan districts of Saugor and Damoh, and in the northern or Vindhyan half of the Jubbulpur district, distress was acute among the hill aborigines who had lost their crops of millet on which they chiefly depend for food-grain. There was also considerable distress among the agriculturists in the open country, as their resources had been exhausted by previous bad seasons. In the wheat-growing valley of the Nerbudda, comprising the southern half of Jubbulpur, Hoshangabad, Narsingpur and Nimar, the failure of the autumn crop and a very small spring crop combined with previous bad seasons to create wide-spread distress. In this fertile tract artificial irrigation is almost unknown. Where the monsoon rains, ordinarily here so certain, fail the cultivator, the loss of crop is necessarily great. The districts of the Satpura plateau—Chhindwara, Seoni, Betul, Mandla, and part of Balaghat—chiefly depend on the early rain crops. In 1896 these failed very generally throughout the plateau and little *rabi** was sown. In this tract, with the exception of the open part of the Chhindwara district where the crops were fairly good, distress was severe, and was heightened by exhaustion of local food stocks, inertness of trade and difficult communications with the lowlands, and consequent great rise in prices. South of the Satpuras the districts of Chanda, Wardha and Nagpur were more favoured with rainfall, the early autumn millets gave a moderate out-turn, and a fair area was sown with wild weather crops. In these districts there was comparatively little distress. There remain the three districts of Sambalpur, Raipur, and Bilaspur, in the Chhattisgarh division, and the Bhandara district in the Nagpur division, in all of which rice is the chief crop. The Sambalpur district and the southern half of the Raipur district had a fair rice harvest, and the cultivators also possessed large stocks from previous years which have been exported throughout the scarcity at great profit to the holders. The northern half of the Raipur district, the whole of the Bilaspur district, and three-fourths of the Bhandara district were severely distressed.

Among the circumstances which have made the famine in the Central Provinces exceptionally severe and widespread are the large aboriginal population, the exhausting effect of two previous bad years, the preponderance of rain crop cultivation, and the absence of large perennial irrigation systems like those which are so beneficial in Upper India. The very immunity from drought which this part of India has enjoyed in the past and the abundance of the average rainfall make drought here especially disastrous.

---

* *Rabi* is the vernacular term for the cold weather crops; *kharif* for the rain crops. In Bengal the early rain crops are known by the name *bhadoi*.

16. In the Punjab the distressed area is returned at 13,000 square miles, with a population of about 3½ millions, but relief on an extensive scale has been confined to the Hissar district. In this district very little of the rain crops or of the cold weather crop came to maturity, the cattle died in large numbers from want of grass and water, while the resources of the people had previously been exhausted by a very bad season in 1895–96. The other districts (Rohtak, Karnal, Umballa, Delhi and Ferozepur) in which relief was required lie in the south and south-east of the province. In all these the autumn and the cold weather crops yielded little, except on irrigated lands. In the Rohtak district the rain crop was half an average one, and the area under cold weather crops was less than one-third of the average acreage. There was no rain here from September to January, except a few showers in September. In the Ferozepur district the unirrigated area sown with cold weather crops was only 193,000 acres against an average of 701,000 acres. By utilising to the full every means of irrigation the cultivators secured 487,000 acres of wet crop against an average of 351,000 acres. But this extension of irrigation did not make up for the loss of crop on the dry lands, though it enabled the district to tide over a drought of exceptional severity. Between April and 31st October only 3 inches of rain fell in this district, the average being 14 inches. The November showers were slight and December was rainless.

The Punjab.

17. In Burma the area affected comprised the whole of one district (Meiktila) and parts of two others (Yamethin and Myingyan), which are situated in the "dry-zone" region of Upper Burma. The rainfall of this region is light and precarious, and droughts have frequently occurred in the past. The population is fortunately sparse, averaging about 100 to the square mile, and the male portion is accustomed to migrate to Lower Burma for some months of each year for harvest work. In 1896–97 there was an almost total failure of crops of all kinds. In 1897 also the rainfall up to the end of August was in great defect and the early crops failed extensively. Matters have since improved, owing to opportune and fairly heavy rain, but distress is expected to continue for some months longer. At no time, however, have the numbers on relief exceeded 35,000, and they have now fallen to 18,000. There has been no difficulty about food supplies, as rice has been freely imported from Lower Burma.

Burma.

18. The whole area of Berar is returned as affected, as relief operations were to some extent required in all the districts. But this somewhat overstates the extent or degree of distress. The autumn crops failed generally to the extent of a half, and the less important cold weather crops are estimated to have yielded only a quarter of the average. But the cultivating population of the Berars is exceptionally prosperous and well-to-do, and is able to tide over a single bad year without great distress. The labouring population has been affected by high prices and want of employment, and in the forest region of the Melghat there was severe distress. The numbers on relief have, however, never exceeded 34,000, and as an indication of the prosperity of the province it may be mentioned that the stocks of grain with the cultivating population at the beginning of the scarcity were believed to be fully a year's supply.

Berar.

19. The affected area in the territories of native states is returned at 82,000 square miles, with a population of 7,000,000. It comprised the Bikanir, Bhurtpur and Dholpur States in Rajputana, and in Central India the northern districts of the Gwalior State, and virtually all the States (of which Rewa is the largest) forming the Baghelkhand and Bundelkhand Agencies, and lying between British Bundelkhand on the north and the Central Provinces on the south. The southern States of Rajputana, the States of Indore and Bhopal, and the southern districts of Gwalior, in Central India, were not sufficiently affected to require relief operations, although they also experienced short harvests. In the Deccan the south-western districts of the Hyderabad State, which lie in the angle between the distressed districts of Kurnool and Bellary in the Madras Presidency and the distressed districts of Dharwar and Bijapur in the Bombay Presidency, were affected in much the same degree as the adjoining British districts.

Native States.

In Bundelkhand and Baghelkhand intense distress prevailed, as in the adjoining districts of British Bundelkhand in the North-Western Provinces and Oudh. There was widespread failure of the autumn crop, and the spring harvest in most parts was miserably poor. The cultivating and labouring classes were reduced to extreme destitution and underwent great privations. There was continued emigation into British territory, which was productive of much anxiety and inconvenience owing to the wanderers crowding on to the nearest relief works and peopling the poor-houses and relief camps on the main lines of communication. The measures of relief adopted by the rulers of the States concerned will be described later on. Here it is sufficient to say that they were not always sufficient to meet the emergency. In Gwalior and Bhurtpur and in the affected parts of Rajputana distress, though severe, was at no time nearly so acute as in Bundelkhand. In Hyderabad the affected districts, owing to preceding good seasons, entered upon the year of drought with large reserves of food-grain in the hands of the cultivators. The labouring classes, however, were thrown out of employment and have severely felt the pressure of high prices.

20. A comparison of the areas and populations affected by the late famine with corresponding figures for previous famines gives the following result. The drought of 1876–78 is considered by the Famine Commissioners to have been the most serious and widespread of any that have occurred in the century.* The area affected in Southern India in those two years was about 200,000 square miles, with a population of 36,000,000. In this area famine was intense in an area of 105,000 square miles, with a population of 19,000,000; severe in an area of 66,000 square miles, with a population of 11,000,000, and slight in an area of 34,000 square miles, with a population of 6,000,000. In 1877–78 a further area of 52,000 square miles in the North-Western Provinces and the Punjab, with a population of 22,000,000, was afflicted by a failure of the rains, though it suffered to a far less degree. In August, 1877, just before the drought broke up, the total area affected in India was about 250,000 square miles, with a population of 58,000,000. In the late famine severe or intense distress extended over an area of about 270,000 square miles, with a population of over 50,000,000, and a further area of 33,000 square miles, with a population of 13,000,000 was so far distressed as to make relief operations necessary. Thus in point of actual extent the late famine affected a wider area than the famine of 1876–77. As regards the area of intense distress it is safe to place in this category about 40,000 square miles in the Central Provinces, with a population of 5,000,000; 3,000 square miles in Oudh, with a population of 2,000,000; 12,000 square miles in British Bundelkhand, with a population of 3,000,000, and 25,000 square miles in Central India, with a population of 3,000,000. This gives a total area of 80,000 square miles in which distress was intense, with a total population of 14,000,000, without including any portion of North Behar or the Deccan or the Hissar district, in the Punjab, in parts of which the Famine Commission's criterion of intense distress—the loss of 75 per cent. of the average harvest of the year—was fully satisfied. As regards therefore the extent of intense famine there is little to choose between the drought of 1876–78 and that of 1896–97. The numbers on relief, if this be any test, have been very much greater on this occasion than in 1876–78, and a very high level of prices has continuously prevailed over a larger area than in that year. Where this year's famine has fortunately differed from the famine of 1876–78 is that the drought has completely broken up, save in the Deccan and Upper Burma, at the end of the first year. Even in the Deccan and Upper Burma the rainfall of September should secure a cold weather crop and place the termination of distress within measurable distance. At no point of time has the crisis been so acute as in August 1877, when Southern India had entered upon its second year of famine and the rains to all appearance had failed in Upper India.

* Famine Commission's Report. Part I, paragraph 75.

III.—The course of prices.

21. Prices are the barometer of scarcity in India. Even when high prices in a locality are occasioned not by local failure of crops, but by failure elsewhere, they mark the beginning of pressure on the landless classes,—the day labourer in the villages and the poorer inhabitants of the towns. From the rainfall of the year 1896–97 to the course of prices in that year is therefore a natural transition. The following return gives the average prices in each month in certain markets of the food-grains most in use in each tract:—

Province and District.			1893.	1894.	1895.	1896. June.	1896. July.	1896. August.	1896. September.	1896. October.	1896. November.	1896. December.	1897. January.	1897. February.	1897. March.	1897. April.	1897. May.	1897. June.	1897. July.	1897. August, first half.
1.—N.W.P. and Oudh.	*Cawnpore*	Wheat	15·62	17·9	16·32	13	13	12·37	9·37	8·31	8·12	8·56	9·12	9·12	9·37	10·44	10·37	9·56	9·94	9·5
		Barley	22·77	21·33	20·31	16	15	14·62	11·25	9·5	9·12	9·25	9·75	10·62	12·25	12·37	12·5	11·25	12	12
		Gram	23·12	23·57	20·34	16·25	15·62	14·75	11	9·62	9·62	10	9·88	9·62	10·5	9·75	9·5	9·12	9·25	8·75
		Jawar	22·54	23·91	19·59	...	...	15·25	11·62	11	10·12	10·37	10·62	10·62	10·37	10·5	...	...	...	...
2.—Punjab.	*Lahore* ...	Wheat	16·12	24·08	18·17	16	14·5	14	11	9·5	8·12	8·5	9·88	8·44	7·97	10·31	12·06	11·78	10·5	10·12
		Barley	26·92	41	31·37	21·5	19·5	19	14	11·5	9·75	9·5	11·12	11	9·88	13·31	13·88	14·69	14	12·62
		Gram	26·46	35·37	25·83	19	17	17	12·5	10·5	9·62	9·88	11·5	10·31	9·94	11·75	11·78	10·84	10·15	9
		Maize	18·42	34·12	23·54	14	16	15	13	12	10·5	10·88	11	11	10·12	10·5	7·25	7·75	9	8·25
3.—Bengal.	*Patna* ...	Rice (common) ...	16·5	15·9	18·42	17	16·37	14·25	12·12	9·88	10·25	10·34	10·25	10·25	10·25	9·37	8·75	8·62	8·12	8
		Barley	22·43	22·79	24·21	21	19·5	17	15	11·5	11	12	12·5	13	14	13·75	13·25	12·5	11·5	12
	Darbhanga	Marua	24·17	23·67	26·23	25·5	26	22·5	20	16·25	15·5	13	12	12	12	11·37	11·12	11	9·62	11
		Maize	22·45	21·08	24·21	22	20	22	17·5	13·25	11·88	10·37	9·88	9·62	...	9	9·5	9	...	8·5
4.—Central Provinces.	*Nagpur* ...	Wheat	15·48	16·61	15·1	13·75	13·75	12·81	12·19	9·69	8·44	9·69	9·37	9·37	9·37	9·06	8·75	8·28	8·12	8·12
		Jawar	18·85	20·11	18·36	17·81	17·81	18·75	18·12	12·81	11·28	14·37	13·44	11·5	10·94	10·09	10·66	8·91	8·91	9·19
	Mandla ...	Wheat	17·33	18·08	15·67	12·62	12·5	10·5	9·25	8·75	9·5	9·5	9	8·25	9	8·25	8	7·5	8·25	8·5
		Gram	21·37	26·67	19·94	13·75	13	12	10·75	10·5	10·5	10·5	10	10	11	10	9·25	7·88	7·88	8·5
	Bilaspur	—Rice...	18·42	18·11	16·76	12·31	12·31	12·31	10·12	9	10	10·37	10·69	10·34	9·12	8·62	8·5	8	7·56	8
	Betul ...	—Jawar	21·87	27·04	18·58	15·53	14·41	14·37	14·37	14·37	10·25	10·25	10·44	9·75	9·06	8·5	8·5	6·75	7·56	8
5.—Bombay.	*Poona* ...	Wheat	11·08	13·52	14·09	12·81	12·81	12·81	11·22	8·12	7·28	7·84	8·12	7·84	6·37	6·66	6·94	6·94	6·94	6·94
		Jawar	17·09	18·27	20·08	20	20	20	18·81	9·97	9·97	9·97	10·56	10·28	9·37	9·37	9·37	9·09	8·25	7·62
	Bijapur	—Jawar	20·56	22·66	27·18	25·19	25·19	25·19	20·69	12·59	9·91	11·25	11·72	11·69	9·88	11·25	10·41	9·06	7·62	7·62
6.—Madras.	*Bellary*	Cholum	21·81	23·87	29·73	31·12	30·62	30·62	25·75	13·12	11·09	13·87	13·12	12·37	11·59	12	11·62	10·72	9·15	8·81
		Ragi	23·4	24·41	30·25	29·12	29·12	29·56	25·72	16·5	13·59	17·44	16	16·5	16	16·5	16·5	15·06	14·12	13·62
		Rice (common) ...	10·55	10·79	10·86	10·81	10·81	10·81	10·25	8·37	7·81	8·91	9·19	9·19	9·19	8·62	8·62	8·12	7·88	7·62

(1) This table, which has been compiled from the *Gazette of India* returns, gives the number of seers, and decimals of seer, purchaseable for Re. 1. 1 seer = 2·057 lbs.
(2) Jowar or Cholum is a large millet, the *Sorghum vulgare*.
(3) Marua or Ragi is a small millet, the *Eleusine coracana*.

22. From this table it will be observed that, compared with the prices prevailing in the three previous years, prices ruled high in the North-Western Provinces in the early part of 1896 before there was any apprehension of the failure of the monsoon rains. The harvests of 1895-96 had been poor in the provinces generally, and in the Bundelkhand districts very bad. The Punjab in 1895-96 also had poor harvests, and prices there in June 1896 were relatively high. In Madras and Bombay harvests had been good, and food-grains in June 1896 were cheap. It will also be observed that the great difference existing in ordinary years between the price of wheat and the commoner grains vanishes in a year of scarcity, and that then all food-grains draw together at the same high level of price.

23. According to the Famine Commission, "in time of very great scarcity "prices of food-grain rise to three times their ordinary amount, so that whereas in "ordinary years the price of the food-grain of the mass of the people may be from "20 to 30 sers the rupee, in time of great scarcity it will rise to 8 or 10 sers "(16 to 20 lbs.) the rupee and even higher." The course of prices during the late famine has been in general conformity with this rule. The cheapest grain purchaseable has for months ruled throughout vast areas at 8 or 10 sers the rupee and even higher. But since the Famine Commission wrote, the price of food grains in ordinary years has risen in India, and only in exceptionally good seasons does the rate of 30 sers to the rupee maintain. In the Punjab 1894 was such a year, and very low prices for the commoner grains prevailed. In Eastern Bengal, one of the most prosperous parts of India, the price of common rice for years past has not exceeded Re. 1 for 15 sers. In 1880-85 from 20 to 30 sers was there the ordinary rate. In the Bombay Deccan the price of the great millet (jowari), which is the staple food of the people, is now more often above than below Re. 1 for 20 sers. The rise in food-grain prices since 1881 is still more remarkable in tracts to which the railway has penetrated. In 1880-84 rice sold at from 30 to 50 sers the rupee in the Chhattisgarh Division of the Central Provinces. The normal price of recent years has been below 20 sers. These facts have to be borne in mind in applying the formula of the Famine Commission to the present circumstances of India. A rate of 8 or 10 sers the rupee, though it still presses heavily on the great mass of the population, can no longer be regarded as a rise of 300 per cent. on the normal price of food-grains. Another peculiarity of the late scarcity is that though prices rose at once in the first days of the drought to famine level, as determined by the Famine Commission, it was only in the worst tracts and in the time of greatest apprehension that they reached the extreme height of former famines. In June and July of 1877 *jowari* rose in the Bijapur District in the Bombay Deccan to 4½ sers the rupee. This year, although the crop failure in Bijapur was as widespread and complete as in 1877, prices have remained steady at between 7 and 9 sers the rupee. In the Central Provinces food grains rose for a fortnight to 5½ sers the rupee in the Mandla District in July last owing to exhaustion of local stocks; but on import being resumed, prices at once fell back to a lower level. High rates were also reached in parts of the Chota Nagpur Division, where local supplies gave out early in the year, and the distances from the railway and large markets are considerable. Here rice, the stape food-grain of the country, has at times touched 4½ and 5 sers for the rupee, and might have risen higher had not the Government by a system of bounties stimulated importation. If such exceptional cases be left out of account, it may be said that a rate of from 7 to 10 sers the rupee has been maintained throughout the greater part of India with singular persistency from the failure of the monsoon in October 1896. The great equality of prices throughout the country was also remarkable. The Meerut Division of the North-Western Provinces had good autumn crops and a good cold weather harvest. But prices have ruled practically as high there as in famine-stricken Bundelkhand. In the Punjab there was only the difference of the railway freight between prices in the most fortunate of the canal districts, where the cold weather crops were nearly up to the average, and in Hissar, where not one acre in five yielded a crop. This universal prevalence of high prices was the cause of much privation amongst the poorer classes, especially the poor classes of towns, outside the areas of local failure of crops. On the other hand, tenants and owners of land in the non-distressed districts have made large profits, and in such

exceptional tracts the poor seem to have been sufficiently provided for by private liberality. In the Madras Districts lower prices have prevailed than elsewhere, as the crops in the south of the Presidency were good. But the tendency has been for the Madras prices to level up to those of the Bombay Deccan, more especially in the later period of the famine.

IV.—Food Stocks.

24. The rapid and extraordinary rise in prices described in the preceding section raises the question whether there was any serious deficiency of food supply in the country. The materials are not sufficient for a full discussion of this most important question, but it cannot be entirely excluded from consideration.

The position of India in ordinary years is that it produces sufficient food for its own requirements, with something to spare for export or for storage. The Famine Commission after a prolonged enquiry came to the conclusion that the annual food grain production of British India (excluding Burma but including Mysore which was then under British rule) was 51,530,000 tons, that its requirements were satisfied by 47,165,000 tons, and that a surplus of 5,165,000 tons was available for export or for storage. Since the Famine Commission wrote the population of the same area has risen from 181 millions to 212 millions, an increase of 17 per cent. The food requirements of this increased population would, on the data employed by the Famine Commission, be 54,308,000 tons. During the same period the area under food grains has risen from 166½ millions of acres to 185 millons, an increase of only 8 per cent. The production of the present food crop area, according to the standard of yield adopted for each province by the Famine Commission, is 56,000,000 tons. On these figures a surplus of only 1,700,000 tons results, in place of the surplus of 5,160,000 tons estimated by the Famine Commission in 1881 as existing in ordinary years. If the Famine Commission's estimate was at all correct, it is difficult to avoid the conclusion that a deficiency in the yield in any year is now more serious than in 1881, since the margin in ordinary years is smaller. Allowance must be made for the greater extension of irrigation during the last decade and for the larger average yield of the areas thus benefited. But the most liberal allowance on this account will not bring the annual surplus above 2,500,000 tons. This estimate receives some confirmation from the statistics of sea exports. The exports of food grains from British India (excluding Burma) to foreign countries have averaged 1¼ millions of tons in the last 10 years and little over 1 million of tons in the last five. If the food production of the country resulted in ordinary years in a surplus much in excess of these figures, the consequent accumulation of stocks would be indicated by a fall in prices. But prices on the whole have tended to rise. In particular years particular provinces no doubt produce food in large excess of their requirements and in excess of the estimated surpluses shown by the Famine Commission. This was the case in the Punjab in 1894-95 and in the Bombay Deccan and Madras in 1895-96, and it was marked by a very low range of prices in those tracts, by exportation from them to other parts of India where harvests had been less bountiful, and by large surplus stocks which have proved very useful in the present famine. But this is not incompatible with the theory that taking the country as a whole its surplus production of food grains in ordinary years is small, and that if the crops in any year are below the average over considerable areas, the year's outturn will fall very seriously below the requirements of the population. In the above survey the food production of Burma and of the Native States of India has been left out of account. As regards the Native States it seems probable that their exportable surplus ordinarily is small. Burma has usually an exportable surplus of from ¾ths of a million to 1½ million tons of rice, most of which finds a market in Europe and the Straits. This year however, a large portion of the Burma surplus was diverted to India and had a very salutory effect in steadying the Indian markets.

Famine Commission's Report, Part I, paragraph 156.

25. To return to the outturn of 1896-97. The crops are known to have failed very seriously over large areas, and elsewhere were below the average. There is thus a strong probability that the production of the year was much below the

requirements of the population. Yet with the exception of 600,000 tons of Burma rice there was no import of food grains from abroad, and there has been no absolute dearth of food. It has always been purchaseable though dear. Accumulated stocks must therefore have been in existence and have made good the deficiency in the year's output. The amount of the deficiency cannot be quantitatively stated. All that can here be done is to indicate approximately, by examination of the effect of the drought on the harvests of each province, the extent to which the year's outturn appears to have been below that of ordinary years.

26. In the *Punjab* the aggregate yield of the autumn and the spring harvests of 1896-97 seems to have been about 25 per cent. or 30 per cent. short of an average crop. In some districts the deficiency was very much greater and in others less than this. Considering the scanty rainfall of the year the result was highly satisfactory, and it could not have been attained were it not that the province is exceptionally well equipped with canals and wells and its agriculturists willing and able to make the fullest use of them. No less than 40 per cent. of the rain crop area and 50 per cent. of the spring crop of 1896-97 was irrigated—percentages higher than have ever been known before. The food grain production of the Punjab is in normal seasons considerably in excess of its requirements. Taking into account the economy in consumption enforced by high prices, the yield of 1896-97, though below the average, probably represented one year's food supply for the province. The food stocks in existence in the province at the beginning of the drought have been estimated to represent 7 months' further supply. Thus the Punjab as a whole has been very fortunately situated. Local deficiencies of food stocks, as in the district of Hissar, have been easily made good by importations from the less affected districts, and grain has been steadily going out of the province to the North-Western Provinces and the Central Provinces.

The *North-Western Provinces and Oudh* were less fortunately situated. These provinces owing to their dense population are not credited with producing a large surplus of food even in ordinarily good years. In 1896–97 the autumn crop as a whole was fully 50 per cent. and the spring crop 33 per cent. below the average. Taking the two crops together the province may be considered to have lost two-fifths of its ordinary harvest outturn. The loss would have been very much greater but for the splendid canal systems which traverse the western and central portions of the North-Western Provinces, under the names of the eastern Jumna Canal, the Agra Canal, and the Ganges Canal, and for the innumerable wells and ponds which stud the face of the country, especially in Eastern and Southern Oudh, and in the eastern districts of the North-Western Provinces. The canals irrigated 3,000,000 acres in the two harvests of 1896–97. The area irrigated by wells and tanks has not yet been returned, but it may be safely said that in very few districts did the spring crops yield much, except on irrigated lands. To irrigation therefore the very fair results of the spring harvest of 1897 must be ascribed. The efforts made by the cultivators to utilise to the fullest possible extent every drop of water and to raise a crop were described by observers as heroic. Still the deficiency in the food production of the year was large. Stocks seem to have been low owing to preceding bad seasons. The statistics of railway traffic show a large continuous import of food grains into the province from the Punjab and Bengal from the first days of the scarcity. Much of the Burma rice found its way to Bundelkhand and Oudh. With the completion of the cold weather harvest the pressure perceptibly eased off in the less distressed parts of the province, and grain moved in large quantities from them to the more distressed tracts.

In *Bengal* the great crop of the year is the winter rice which occupies 31 million acres in a total food crop area of 53 million acres. The food crops harvested in the spring occupy 9½ million acres, and the early rain crops of rice and millets 12¾ million acres. The yield of the late rice crop in 1896-97 is returned at under half an average crop, a deficiency of about 8 or 9 million tons of food. The early rain crops of 1896 were 40 per cent. below the average yield. The spring harvest of 1897 was an average one. The agricultural returns of Bengal are less exact than in other parts of India, and it is possible that the crop failure was not quite as great as reported. But even in that case, the production of the year cannot well be placed above two-thirds of the average outturn. This would be much below the requirements of the population for the twelve months. In the distressed districts of North Behar local stocks were soon exhausted and imports have been on a large scale. Large quantities of Burma rice went there. Elsewhere there must evidently have been considerable reserves of food. Not a few districts have continuously exported and have shown no signs of exhaustion.

In the *Central Provinces* the outturn in 1896–97 seems to have been fully 55 per cent. below the ordinary yield. With average harvests the province is estimated to produce about 3¼ million tons of food-grains, of which from 300,000 to 400,000 tons are in excess of its requirements. This year the outturn fell below its actual requirements by about 1,000,000 tons. The deficiency must have been chiefly met from food stocks existing in the province, as the imports from outside have not been large. Within the province grain has moved freely from the less distressed districts to the more distressed ones. Great economy of consumption has also been practised under the stress of acute distress.

In *Bombay* the Deccan districts enjoyed two good years immediately preceding 1896, and on the estimates of the local Agricultural Department had in that period accumulated reserves of food equivalent to a 9 months' supply. It was fortunate that this was so, for the food-grain outturn of the year in the affected districts was little, if anything, over one-fourth of the ordinary yield. Outside the affected area Sind had average harvests, while Guzerat was somewhat in defect. The total outturn of the Bombay Presidency in 1896–97 may be put at five-eights of the production of an ordinary year, and consequently was less than 12 months' requirements of the population.

In *Madras* the outturn of the distressed area in the Deccan may perhaps be put at one-quarter of the average; and in Ganjam and Vizagapatam the outturn was short by probably 50 per cent. Elsewhere the deficiency was not great, and as the distressed areas were relatively small, the year's outturn of the Presidency was probably within 20 per cent. of the normal. Stocks also were large. Prices have been lower than elsewhere, and the grain exports to other Provinces have exceeded the imports. Madras therefore has not been in serious difficulty about its food-supplies.

In the *Berars* the autumn crop which there occupies a much larger area than the spring crop was said to be short by 50 per cent.; and the spring crop by 75 per cent. This is probably an over estimate of loss. The cultivators were said to have had a year's supply of food-grains in hand, and though prices have been high, there seems at all times to have been sufficient food in the province.

Regarding the *Native States* in which distress has prevailed, it is only possible to speak in general terms about their food production and requirements. In the Nizam's Dominions the distressed districts had, like the Bombay and Madras Deccan country, enjoyed good seasons up to 1896, and entered on the scarcity with large stocks of grain. Much of this was drawn away to British districts in the first months of the drought, and then holders of grain took alarm and refused to sell. Prices reached a very high level in parts of the State, but there is evidence that considerable reserves still exist. In Bundelkhand and Baghelkhand the year's production of food must have been much below the requirements of the population, as the harvests were as bad as in British Bundelkhand. On the relief works in Rewah considerable quantities of Burma rice were sold, and despite of the prejudices which as a novelty it excited it found its way into remote village marts. The Gwalior and Dholpur States must also have been short of supplies, as they imported grain largely from the Meerut Division of the North-Western Provinces and Oudh, and from Rajputana. The Rajputana States on the other hand had for the most part fair harvests and considerable stocks, and were able to export.

27. Summarising the results of this investigation as regards British India, the table below indicates that the food-outturn of British India (excluding Burma) in 1896–97 was about one-third below that of ordinary years. This represents a deficiency of about 18 or 19 million tons. The consumption of the people under the stress of high prices has unquestionably been reduced, and a portion of the

deficiency has in this way been covered. The rest has been made good by reserve stocks, and by the import of about 600,000 tons of rice from Burma.

Province.	Population by present census.	Normal food crop area.	Defect in yield of 1896–97 below the normal.
		Acres.	
1. Punjab	20,800,000	22,000,000	25 per cent.
2. North-Western Provinces and Oudh ...	47,000,000	36,000,000	40 ,,
3. Bengal	71,000,000	53,000,000	33 ,,
4. Central Provinces	10,700,000	14,500,000	55 ,,
5. Berar	2,900,000	4,000,000	40 ,,
6. Bombay	18,800,000	23,000,000	35 ,,
7. Madras	36,000,000	27,500,000	20 ,,
Total	*207,200,000	180,000,000	33 ,,

* The exclusion of Mysore accounts for the difference between these figures and those given in paragraph 24

V.—The first period of the Famine—Alarm and Preparations.

North-Western Provinces and Oudh.

28. The first premonitory report of the impending trouble came from the North-Western Provinces and Oudh. On the 30th September 1896 the Lieutenant-Governor informed the Government of India that since the beginning of the month increasingly unsatisfactory reports of the condition of the people and the prospects of the crops had been received from his officers. The rains, it was said, had practically ceased just when they were most wanted. Very serious damage had already been done to the autumn or *kharif* crops. If sufficient rain should fall before the middle of October, it was anticipated that the *kharif* still standing might be saved, and that the usual *rabi* area would be sown. If no rain were to fall the outlook would be very serious. The provinces had already suffered from two successive years of bad harvests. The people were crippled in resources and their stocks of grain exhausted. Prices were very high. and were still rising. Wheat was selling at 9 to 10 seers the rupee, and barley at 12 sirs, prices which represented a rise of 50 per cent. on those ruling in the early part of the year. In anticipation of relief measure on an extensive scale being necessary, the programmes of relief works were being carefully revised. A list of railway projects was given, the earthwork of which would afford useful and beneficial employment for famine labour. To this report was added a copy of the instructions which the local Government had addressed to district officers, directing them to institute special inquiries in each subdivision as to the actual condition of the *kharif* crops and the prospects of sowings for the *rabi* crops, and to report the result, together with estimates of the maximum number of persons for whose relief provision would be required, by the end of October. Authority at the same time had been given to them, in case distress appeared, to open public works under ordinary labour conditions to test the pressure on the people. They were also enjoined to complete in advance all the preparations prescribed by the Famine Code for the methodical and effective administration of relief.

29. This preliminary report was followed on the 23rd November by a letter setting out very fully the situation as then developed and describing the measures which the local Government had adopted for dealing with it. This letter is remarkable for the accuracy with which it anticipated the extent and nature of the distress which would occur, and for the forethought with which the detailed plan of operations that has been followed with complete success and very little variation had been prepared. It began by reporting that no improvement in the outlook had occurred. October like September had been practically rainless. The only portion of the province which had escaped injury was the Meerut Division, where heavy rainfall in July and August had successfully carried the crops

through the subsequent dry months, and the parts of the Agra Division which are protected by canals. In the rest of the provinces the failure of the *kharif* crop varied from a loss of one-fourth in certain localities to a loss of three-fourths and over in others, the failure being greatest in those districts in which rice was most largely grown. The tract most affected lay between the Ganges and the Gogra, and included the greater part of Oudh and the district of Azamgarh. With this area Bundelkhand was also classed as, although its *kharif* in four districts out of five was returned as one-third of an average harvest, it had already suffered from famine. The worst area thus arrived at comprised 35,000 square miles, with a population of 15¾ millions. With regard to the prospects of the *rabi* crop the sowings were estimated at 58 per cent. of the normal area cropped, ranging from over 70 per cent. in the Meerut and Rohilkhand Divisions to 42 per cent. in the Allahabad Division. Much, it was said, depended on rain falling in December and January. In the worst area famine was anticipated whether there were winter rains or not. In the area of less serious crop failure, comprising about 20,000 square miles with a population of 11¼ millions, there would be much distress deepening in particular localities into famine. In the remaining area no general relief would be required. As to food supplies, confidence was expressed that there were considerable stocks of grain in the country and that food would not fail as long as there was money to buy it. Prices were, it was true, phenomenally high, and presented "many of the features, notably that of approaching equality between "the prices of the coarsest and the best food grains, which characterise famine "times." But trade was active, and the Lieutenant-Governor strongly expressed his opinion that it would be equal to any probable emergency, and that nothing should be done to interfere with its free play.

30. The relief measures which had already been started were then described. Advances had been liberally made to cultivators for the construction of wells and the purchase of seed, and over 200,000 temporary wells had been thus constructed for irrigating the winter crop. Land revenue to the extent of 80 lacs of rupees (£x. 800,000) had been suspended. Programmes of large public works, chiefly the construction and repair of roads, calculated to employ 3,000,000 labourers for three months, were ready, and nearly 100,000 relief labourers were already employed. These works were to be managed by the Department of Public Works. Certain railway projects were also proposed with the same object to the Government of India for early sanction. In addition to these works, lists of small village works were being drawn up, which it was proposed to utilise for the purpose of drawing the people from large works back to their homes at the approach of the hot weather and employing them in their own villages. Poor-houses had been opened for the reception of waifs and strays, and relief circles formed and circle officers appointed in each distressed district for the purpose of administering relief in their homes to women debarred by custom from appearing in public, and to men of respectable classes unaccustomed to manual labour, to whom such relief is admissible. It has been already said of this programme that in few respects only were departures from it necessary. These departures may here be conveniently noticed. For various reasons few of the railway projects recommended by the local Government could be utilised as relief works, and relief labour has been practically confined to road-making and road repairs. Small village works have proved less useful than was anticipated, and large works have been found necesssary throughout the famine. Gratuitous relief, as time went on, was largely expanded, and embraced not only the classes unaccustomed to work or to appear in public, but the aged, the young and the feeble of the labouring classes.

Bengal.

31. The Government of Bengal in October 1896 submitted to the Government of India two preliminary reports from the Commissioner of the Patna Division on the condition and prospects of the crops of his division. The Commissioner reported that the winter rice crop was withering daily from want of rain, and that prices were rising fast. These reports were followed in November by a more complete account of the situation both in Behar and in the rest of Bengal. It was remarked that "all known famines in Bengal and Orissa have been rice "famines. In Behar and Northern Bengal the *bhadoi* and *rabi* crops may be the "turning point between famine and no famine, but even there the immediate cause

"of scarcities and famines has always been the failure of the winter rice crop." For this crop rain is required in September and October. In September 1896 the only considerable fall occurred about the middle of the month, which saved, though it failed to fully restore, the crop in most districts except in east Behar. In parts of six districts in Central Bengal and Orissa, a deficiency of 50 per cent. of an average crop was anticipated. These tracts, however, were not considered to give cause for anxiety, except that prices were everywhere extraordinarily high. In Behar the Commissioner put the probable yield of the rice crop for the whole Patna Division at not more than a quarter of the average yield. An area of 4,300 square miles with a population of $3\frac{1}{2}$ millions was estimated by him to be likely to require relief, and relief would be necessary for about 5 per cent. of this population, or 170,000 persons. The Government of Bengal thought this estimate of relief too low, as no doubt it was. The crop-failure in Behar was, in its opinion, as great as in 1873–74, while the circumstances of the people were little improved. "The "population is extremely dense, and the great majority of the people are much "poorer than in most other parts of these provinces. The ordinary wages of "agricultural labour are extremely low, being for able-bodied and agricultural "labourers only from $1\frac{1}{2}$ to $2\frac{1}{2}$ annas the day, and they have, owing partly to the "growth of population, and partly to the influence of custom, remained practically "unaltered for the past 20 years or more, while the prices of food grains have "increased largely during the same period." But what caused the Bengal Government most anxiety was the possibility of a serious deficiency in the food supply of Behar. According to its calculations, the outturn of the three harvests of the year in the Patna Division, together with stocks in hand (assumed to be equal to three months' supply), would be below the year's requirements of the division by 550,000 tons. Where the difference was to come from and whether private trade would be equal to supplying the deficit were questions which the Government of Bengal was very doubtful about, though it inclined to the opinion that by importations of rice from Burma or of wheat from America private trade would meet the food wants of the Province.

32. It may be noticed that the Commissioner, though he furnished the estimates of crop-yield on which the local Government based its calculations, took a hopeful view of the situation. Comparing it with the situation in 1873–74 he thought that the material prosperity of the division had increased, that owing to good years the people were in better condition than in 1873, and that the two crops (*bhadoi* and *kharif*) of which there was fairly certain knowledge were better than in 1873, except in Muzaffarpur and Saran. He saw no reason to fear that the third crop (*rabi*) would not be as good as in 1873–74, when it varied from a half to a three-quarters crop. In that case the Patna, Shahabad and Gya districts would have a total outturn from the three harvests approaching or exceeding half the normal yield. In Champaran, Darbhanga and Muzaffarpur the *rabi* was comparatively unimportant, and owing to the serious deficiency in the *bhadoi* and *kharif* crops he considered the outlook there to be serious. He remarked, however, that since 1873–74 an entire revolution had been wrought in all the conditions of famine relief in Behar by the immense development of communications. In 1873–74 there was only one railway in Behar, and that ran through the two southern districts of Patna and Shahabad. In 1896 there was at least one line of rail in each district, and in the division 589 miles were open. In 1873-74 the Sone canals had

Comparative outturn in annas furnished by the Commissioner.*

—	1873.		1896–97.	
	Bhadoi.	*Kharif.*	*Bhadoi.*	*Kharif.*
Patna	4	2	10	9
Gya	8	6	12	8
Shahabad	4	2	$7\frac{1}{2}$	4
Saran	$10\frac{3}{5}$	$1\frac{2}{3}$	6	3
Champaran	10	2	$8\frac{1}{2}$	$3\frac{1}{3}$
Muzaffarpur	$11\frac{4}{5}$	$4\frac{5}{8}$	5	3
Darbhanga	9	$2\frac{3}{4}$	8	5

Relative areas under each main crop in 1896–97.

—	*Bhadoi.*	*Kharif.*	*Rabi.*
Patna	20·5	43·4	36·0
Gya	9·6	65·9	24·5
Shahabad	7·6	44·3	48·1
Saran	31·5	30·1	38·4
Champaran	35·0	43·9	21·0
Muzaffarpur	24·1	45·6	30·2
Darbhanga	21·2	57·7	21·0

* A 16 annas (= Re. 1) yield is taken in Indian agricultural estimates to represent an average crop: and 8 anna crop is thus half an average crop. A 20 annas crop is a full or bumper crop.

not been opened. In 1896 they supplied water communication for many miles. In 1873–74 there were no steam ferries in the division. Now they were frequent. Lastly in 1873–74 the number of roads open were a mere fraction of what they were in 1896. In the whole division 12,500 miles of road were now open. He rightly concluded that all these charges would immensely facilitate, and render vastly less expensive, the supply of grain and the execution of all operations connected with the relief of distress.

33. In December, on the Lieutenant-Governor visiting Behar, the details of the scheme of relief were settled. The distressed tracts were blocked out into relief charges and relief circles. A charge contained an area of about 200 to 300 square miles with a population of about 250,000 persons: and a circle an area of about 30 to 40 square miles with a population of about 25,000 to 30,000 persons. To such of the charges as could not be officered by Assistant Magistrates, Police Officers and Deputy Collectors, young indigo planters specially employed for the occasion were appointed. In the three districts of Champaran, Darbhanga and Muzaffarpur, where the failure of the rice crop was greatest, 15 charges and 66 circles (to be increased eventually to 31 charges and 197 circles) were immediately formed. With regard to relief works, all large works were to be placed directly under the Department of Public Works, and all others managed by the Civil authorities. A list of large works, including several canal and drainage schemes and two railways, was drawn up, but as the event proved, it was not till a late stage of the scarcity that work could be commenced on them, and in the earlier months the relief workers were mainly employed on small scattered works, mostly village tanks, managed by the charge Superintendents and their subordinates. The Superintendents were also the officers responsible for seeking out the destitute poor in the villages within their charges, and placing respectable women and others, who were unable to labour and ashamed to beg and had no relatives to maintain them, on gratuitous relief in their homes.

To stimulate sowings for the cold weather crop a bonus of one rupee was granted to cultivators for each earthen well sunk by them for irrigation purposes. Money advances free of interest were also offered to landowners and others for undertaking in their own villages the excavation of tanks and the execution of other petty improvements, and thereby providing employment to the people. As Behar enjoys a permanent settlement, no suspension of the land revenue demand was proposed.

34. In these preliminary arrangements for relief in Bengal one or two special features may be noticed. The charge and circle organization was on a much larger and more expensive scale than in any other province and had a much larger European element. This is probably inevitable in Bengal in the absence of the subdivisional and village revenue establishments entertained in temporarily settled Provinces. The prominence given to gratuitous village relief in the duties assigned to this special staff, and the reliance placed on numerous small relief works close to the homes of the people, are also noteworthy. All these feature are found in the administration of the Behar famine of 1873–74. The anxiety felt lest the food-supply should run short and the discussion which afterwards ensued between the local and the supreme Governments as to assisting the trade to import also recall the Behar famine. It is interesting to observe this general tendency in each province to work on the administrative lines of its last great famine. Notwithstanding the levelling influences of the Famine Commission and the Famine Codes the respective relief systems of Madras and Bombay in the late famine presented distinctive features, and these can readily be traced back to the relief methods respectively adopted in each Presidency in the great famine of 1876–78.

The Punjab.

35. The first report from the local Government of the Punjab, written in the third week in November, described the situation in very sombre colours. The rain crops in the south and south-east of the Provinces had extensively failed, and unless rain fell before the end of the year the cold weather crop would also fail. The rise in prices was everywhere causing uneasiness. Actual distress so far was confined to Hissar and adjoining districts, but active preparations throughout

the province to encounter famine were necessary and were being made. As events turned out, these apprehensions proved to be exaggerated. Rain fell in good quantities in December and January, the *rabi* crops in the canal tracts were extremely good, and the *rabi* as a whole was probably within 25 per cent. of the normal outturn. In Hissar and in parts of Rohtak there was severe distress and relief works on an extensive scale were here required. Elsewhere the people maintained themselves without resort to State aid to an unexpected degree, and in the canal tracts the landowning and cultivating classes made large profits through the high prices of grain.

The Punjab Government in its relief measures was fortunate to have ready several large works of permanent utility on which it could employ relief labour. In the Hissar district the Gaggar canal and in the Gujrat district the Jhelum canal were thus utilised. Employment was also found on the earthwork of several projected railway lines. The labourers were generally of a robust type, capable of doing a full day's work, and it is believed that the greater part of the expenditure on relief works in this province during the late famine has returned good value in the form of public works of permanent utility.

The Central Provinces.

36. A premonitory report from the Chief Commissioner of the Central Provinces reached the Government of India in the last week of October. The Chief Commissioner in reporting that the rains had failed since the beginning of September in almost every district of the province was unable as yet to state definitely the extent of damage sustained by the rain-crops or the probabilities of successful cold weather sowings. The emergency however appeared to him to be one "much in excess of any which have previously been experienced in the provinces." What made the situation more serious was that "the three previous years had "been in a great part of the province not years of full crops, and in the three "districts of Saugor, Damoh, and Jubbulpur they had been years of widespread "failure of the important *rabi* harvest." Up to August the rains had been favourable, and the cultivators in the expectation of a good harvest had parted with much of their surplus produce, which had been exported to other provinces where prices were higher. Prices in the provinces had now gone up with a bound : and "after "four years of hardship and short harvests, the agriculturists find themselves in "face of a prospect of some pressure which cannot be expected to slacken until "the next monsoon, it may be hoped, brings back normal weather conditions. "The cumulative force of these adverse circumstances makes the position one "of great gravity." A provisional grant of five lacs for starting relief works was asked for and was given. In November a further grant of 10 lacs was asked for with the object of giving advances to agriculturists for irrigation tanks and other similar works of improvement in certain districts, especially in the rice country of Chhattisgarh, which would furnish employment to the people in the neighbourhood of their homes. "The money spent will be recovered with "interest, the people will be kept from wandering and starvation, villages will "be held together, and cultivation will be rendered secure instead of precarious." Before this application was acceded to some discussion took place as to the restrictions which should surround such expenditure. It was explained to the Chief Commissioner that in a time of financial pressure the Government of India could not find funds for advances for land improvements except under conditions that would ensure that the expenditure actually operated to give relief to persons in distressed tracts who required relief. Similar instructions were given to other local Governments, and throughout the famine have been strictly adhered to by the Government of India in making or refusing allotments for advances for land improvements.

37. In the middle of December the Chief Commissioner reported fully on the situation. The *kharif* was in no district better than half an average crop. The *rabi* crops had germinated better than had been expected, but the area sown was less than usual and some sowings had failed. As the position of each district greatly depended on the character of the harvests of the three preceding years they fell conveniently into the groups given in the table below :—

		A.			B.			C.				D.							
												Poor.					Bad.		
		Sambalpur.	Nimar.	Chhindwara.	Warda.	Nagpur.	Chanda.	Raipur.	Bilaspur.	Betul.	Mandla.	Seoni.	Narsingpur.	Hoshangabad.	Bhandara.	Balaghat.	Jubbulpur.	Damoh.	Saugor.
Estimated anna out-turn of current *kharif*.	...	10	8	5	8	8	8	4	5	4	3	4	6	5	6	3	5	6	5
Proportion of *kharif* to *rabi* area.	*Kharif*	98	87	58	60	50	66	69	61	61	67	48	37	27	63	75	48	46	38
	Rabi	2	13	42	40	50	34	31	36	39	33	52	63	73	37	25	52	54	62
Present prospect of spring crop.	...		Poor.	Good.	Good.	Good.	Good.	Good.	Good.	Poor.	Good.	Good.	Fair.	Fair.	Good.	Good.	Good.	Fair.	Bad.

Groups A and B gave little cause for immediate anxiety, as past harvests had been good or fair and the present harvest was less deficient than elsewhere. In group C the crops of 1895–96 had been good, but the poor yield of the standing *kharif* made some distress certain, especially in Mandla. In group D the situation owing to three bad years, the badness of the *kharif* crop, and the prospect of a poor spring harvest in the Nerbadda districts, where *rabi* is the principal crop, was very serious. "The great majority of the classes in the provinces who will suffer most "are almost entirely dependent on the autumn crops—rice, *juar*, and the smaller "millets. Nearly all their land is cropped with these grains, and when these fail, "as they have this year almost everywhere failed, the most plentiful outturn of "wheat and grain is, apart from its effect in lowering the general price of food "stuffs, of little or no benefit to the people." "We must," the Chief Commissioner continued, "be prepared to face continued and general distress till well on in July "or August. In some parts, notably Saugor, Jubbulpur, Balaghat and parts of "Damoh, past years have been so bad, and the people are so depressed and "impoverished by the calamities of successive seasons, that it will take at least a "year of renewed agricultural prosperity to make the poorest classes independent "of Government relief."

38. The scheme of relief contemplated the opening of village works by the civil authorities in all localities where scope for such works existed, as the first stage in the organization of famine relief. The main thing to be done, it was thought, was to keep the people on their land and to provide sufficient work and food for them near their homes to prevent their throwing up their holdings before better times came round. As distress deepened and the number of persons to be relieved grew, large road works were to be opened under the management of the Public Works Department. For the provision of gratuitous relief, poor-houses had been established at centres. These were to be supplemented by more numerous relief centres brought nearer the homes of the people, with small works attached to them for enforcing a task on applicants for relief capable of doing light work. Gratuitous relief in the homes of the people might eventually have to be organized, but this was thought not to be an urgent matter.

39. This scheme is open to criticism as being adapted to a much lighter calamity than that which actually had befallen the provinces. Distress speedily outran the village works and the poor-houses on which reliance was placed. The relief centres and the poor-house population grew to unmanageable dimensions. As events showed, it would have been better had large relief works under the Department of Public Works been started, and village relief organized, at an earlier date. Unforseen delays occurred in the publication of the departmental programme and the organization of the work-establishments. Village relief could not be effectively administered by the district staffs until they were reinforced by British military officers lent for the purpose by the Military Department, and this took time. The order in which the districts were placed with reference to the degree of distress anticipated in each has proved generally correct, except that as time went on the centre of distress shifted from the Nerbadda Valley to the rice districts of Bilaspur and Raipur, and the plateau districts of Betul, Mandla and Seoni in the Satpura range.

Bombay.

40. A brief intimation of extensive crop failure in the Deccan and Southern Mahratta country was made by the Bombay Government in November. The full report was delayed till January, as a good fall of rain towards the end of November was thought to have materially altered the outlook and rendered comparatively useless the calculations previously made. The area reported to be affected was about 42,000 square miles and comprised the whole or portions of eight districts, with a population of 6¾ millions. It was stated that the *kharif* crops, where they had not absolutely failed (as in Bijapur and Sholapur), had yielded but one-quarter of an average crop: that large areas had been sown with *rabi* chiefly after the November rain: and that the intensity of the distress in each district depended entirely on the outturn of these crops. It was feared that owing to subsequent dry weather the crop sown after the November rain would, except in favoured localities, come to nothing. Prices were extraordinarily high and the pressure on the poorer classes was already severe. There were 167,000 persons already on relief works, and the numbers were rapidly increasing. It was proposed to concentrate labour as much as possible on a few large works and to restrict village works to persons who for various reasons could not leave their homes. There was a keen demand for advances for wells among the agricultural classes, and it was considered that much employment could thus be economically provided. Steps were being taken to open poor-houses, and gratuitous relief was already being given on a small scale in villages to persons unable to labour. The condition of the cattle, owing to the scarcity of fodder, was very serious. Numbers had already died or had been sold for slaughter in Bijapur and Sholapur. The people were being urged to take their cattle to the forests where there was grazing to be had. And to provide for cattle which could not thus be moved the Forest Department had arranged to cut and press grass and place it in depôts at the railway stations. A prominent feature of the distress in the Presidency was the large number of weavers in need of relief. In some towns there were thousands reported to be in search of employment. The great majority of these the local Government considered would require no special provision and could find employment on the ordinary relief works. Only to such as were deemed incapable of thus gaining a livelihood was semi-gratuitous employment in their own craft to be given.

Bijapur.	Nasik.
Sholapur.	Satara.
Belgaum.	Ahmednagar.
Poona.	Khandesh.

41. The decision in this scheme of relief to depend on large works professionally managed has been consistently adhered to with excellent results. The unnecessary expansion of relief which follows the opening of numerous small works was avoided and a very useful distance test was thereby indirectly applied. On the works hutting accommodation was provided for the workers, and as a further test residence upon the work has in some cases been made compulsory. The special fodder arrangements appear to have proved useful. A very large quantity of pressed grass was placed in the districts by the Forest Department, and was disposed of at prices which covered all outlay. Special relief to weavers sank to very small proportions. When it was found that they readily took to employment on the ordinary relief works, and physically improved through the labour, the Bombay Government ceased to make special arrangements for the weaver class, and left it to municipalities in which weavers were numerous to do so from municipal funds if they thought fit. On the recommendation of the Bombay Government the Imperial Legislative Council passed an Act (XII. of 1897) enabling municipal corporations to borrow money for this object. This Act, however, has been very sparingly resorted to by municipalities in Bombay Presidency, as it was found that the cost of the relief proposed to be given was out of all proportion to the number of persons to be relieved.

42. The fears of the local Government that such of the *rabi* crops as were sown after the November rain would, except where irrigated, fail to come to anything proved correct. In February and March the Director of the Agricultural Department after visiting the affected districts reported on their condition and the state of the crops. Of Sholapur he wrote: "Up to November large areas remained "altogether unsown. In that month rain fell heavily in the northern and central "portions of the district with the result that even more than the usual areas were

"sown with *rabi*. The crops on these, though germinating admirably, have come "to nothing but growth from 12 to 18 inches high, which will yield nothing "but a very little fodder for cattle." In Bijapur all vestiges of these November crops had disappeared. "It is difficult to conceive anything more distressing "than the appearance of the district as it presented itself to the eye of the observer "entering it from the north in the month of January. Except in the neighbour- "hood of wells and of the rivers, there was scarcely a blade of green to be "discerned. In the neighbouring parts of the Sholapur district the November "rain had encouraged the cultivators to sow large areas, and the land was covered "with the deceitful promise of a *rabi* crop. In Bijapur the country was as bare "as the palm of the hand." Bijapur and Sholapur were the worst districts. Bijapur virtually had no harvest at all, neither *kharif* or *rabi*, the total yield of the year representing less than one month's food for the population. In the seven Deccan districts inspected the total food-production of the year was returned at only one-fourth of the normal outturn.

Madras.

43. The first report of the Revenue Board which the Madras Government transmitted in November 1896 foreshadowed a widespread failure of crops in the northern districts, especially in the rice-tracts of Ganjam, and in the Deccan and parts of the Central districts. The deficiency in the September and October rainfall was very serious. The tract where the deficiency was greatest comprised a broad belt of country traversing the four Deccan districts of Bellary, Kurnool, Anantapur and Cuddapah—districts which are habitually liable to drought. The harvests of the two previous years had been good, and prices in the Deccan had in June 1896 fallen to the low level of the years preceding the great famine of 1876. Large stocks had accumulated, and but for the scarcity prevailing throughout India the province would have been exceptionally well able to withstand a bad year. But from September grain had been drained from it to Northern India, and prices had advanced by leaps and bounds under the influence of this export and from the reluctance of the cultivators to part with their stocks. Prophecies were current of a fatal three years' cycle of drought, and every well-to-do ryot locked up his remaining store of grain. The poorer classes were already hard pressed. There was little employment in the fields, and the immediate opening of relief works was necessary. The situation was said to be outside the experience of the present generation in famine administration. "Hitherto," wrote the Board, "it has been held that scarcity rates and famine "were the results of the failure of two or more seasons. In the present case the "failure of a single season has resulted in warning or scarcity rates, and for the "poorer classes, which habitually have to buy grain, the latter mean distress and "famine, unless their condition is alleviated."

44. In December the Revenue Board were able to report that heavy rain in the last week of November, followed by a copious north-east monsoon in the southern half of the Presidency, had materially reduced the scarcity area, and had brought about a substantial fall in prices. The affected area was now confined to the belt of country in the Deccan, with a population of $1\frac{1}{4}$ millions, and to parts of the Ganjam and Vizagapatam districts. Relief works in the form of road-repairs had been opened by the district authorities. On relief works and in kitchens about 20,000 persons were receiving relief, but the numbers were not increasing. The people were generally in good condition. The weaver class, a class which is very numerous in the Madras Presidency, was specially distressed owing to slackness of trade and absence of demand for textile goods, and relief at their own trade had been organized for weavers in Bellary and Cuddapah. No gratuitous relief in the homes of the people had as yet been found necessary. In Ganjam test-works had failed to attract labour. In the Deccan, fodder for the cattle was very scarce, and large numbers had been driven off to the Mysore pastures. Compared, however, with other parts of India the affected area in the Madras Presidency appeared from the report to be relatively small. Nor was it at first anticipated that relief on a large scale would be necessary. In the financial estimates for 1896–97 a sum of only 25 lacs for expenditure on famine relief in Madras was provided. But from April 1897 relief rapidly expanded, the expenditure soon outran the 25 lacs, and at the end of July when rain still held off in the south of India there were more persons on relief in Madras than in any other province.

In April the labour task was reduced and the daily wage raised by the local Government in the belief that the conditions of relief hitherto prevailing had been too stringent. Gratuitous relief in the homes of the people was also commenced on an extensive scale, and increased provision made for the special relief of weavers at their trade. To this change of policy the rapid growth of the numbers on relief must in a large measure be ascribed. It will be seen in the sequel that the Madras Government recognised that liberality had gone too far, and as the agricultural outlook improved it took steps to restrict relief within proper bounds.

Native States.

45. In Central India the probability of severe distress occurring in many of the States of Bundelkhand and Baghelkhand was recognised early in October 1896 by the Governor-General's Agent. Bad seasons had been experienced for three years, and many of the States, through no fault of their own, were at the end of their resources. The condition in Rewa, the largest State in Baghelkhand, was found to be very bad, and in Bundelkhand the population of the small States forming that Agency was much distressed. The question of funds was reported by the Governor-General's Agent to be very serious. In the Bundelkhand Agency but six out of twenty-three States had been able to make their own relief arrangements. As funds in the other States were exhausted, he obtained from the Government of India a loan of two lakhs on their behalf to keep the people alive. Shortly after this His Highness the Maharaja Sindhia of Gwalior volunteered to lend money to distressed States through British officers, and after the fullest enquiry and consideration the Governor-General's Agent was authorised to arrange such loans on the basis of interest at 4 per cent guaranteed by the British Government. These loans were to be made subject to the conditions that the resources of the applicant State were exhausted, that the Chief agreed to be guided by the Political Agent in famine matters, and agreed also that his State would be liable to be taken under direct management by the Indian Government on his failure to repay the loan. This arrangement has worked very well. The loans have been of invaluable assistance to the poorer States, while the conditions on which they have been made were well calculated to bring home to the rulers their responsibilities and to induce them to study and enforce economy. The loans were confined to States within the Central India Agency. Outside that Agency the States in which relief measures were needed were comparatively wealthy and did not require such assistance.

46. To advise the States in the administration of famine relief, to see that relief was being given wherever wanted, and that it was given on right principles, an officer, Lieutenant-Colonel A. P. Thornton, of the Political Department, was deputed to visit them in order. Bikanir was first visited, as complaints had been made by the Government of the Punjab that subjects of that State were crowding on to relief works in Punjab districts. From Bikanir he proceeded to Bhartpur and Dholpur, two other States in the Rajputana Agency, and thence to Gwalior. Bundelkhand and Baghelkhand. This tour proved very useful to the States concerned, and also fully informed the Government of India of the situation in each State. In the most affected States Assistant Political Officers were given to the Political Officer in charge, to enable him the more effectively to keep himself informed of the progress of relief and to advise the States. But care was at the same time taken not to impair in any way the responsibility of each State for providing for the relief of its subjects. Very praiseworthy efforts were in many cases made by the Chiefs, and a great deal of good work was done, though, as might be expected, in a less systematic way than the Famine Codes of British India contemplate. In the most distressed tracts relief measures occasionally lagged behind the requirements of the case, and the fact was at once proclaimed by the migration of the subjects of the State in troops to adjoining British districts. In the Nizam's Dominions serious distress was not at first apprehended, as heavy rain in November had done much good to the crops and had encouraged the cultivators to sow more land for a late crop. But as December and January went by without rain, the November sowings came to nothing, food became dear, and the agricultural labourers were without employment. The Nizam's Government promptly recognised the situation, and opened relief works, and suspended payment of the land-revenue, in the distressed tracts.

VI.—The second period. From the commencement of relief operations to the close of the spring harvest.

Growth of distress.

47. During this period the fate of the cold weather crops was decided and the distressed tracts became more distinctly defined. It has been already said that the out-turn of these crops was much below the average, partly because the areas sown were less and partly because sowings on unirrigated lands either failed to germinate or gave a very poor return. Thus the inequalities between field and field and between district and district in the matter of yield were much greater than in ordinary years. In the Bundelkhand districts and in Hissar, where there is very little artificial irrigation and where little rain fell during the winter months, the harvest was miserable and added little to local food stocks. Their exhaustion was seen in a continuous import of grain from other districts. In the Central and Northern Punjab, in the canal districts of the North-Western Provinces, and in parts of Oudh and Behar, much of the crop was good. From there grain was drawn to the distressed districts, and this demand, conjoined with the reluctance of the cultivators to sell, kept prices in these tracts up to famine level. In the Central Provinces the winter crop of 1896–97 occupied only three-fifths of its usual area and much of it was poor. Here also the spring harvest failed to replenish depleted local stocks or to bring down prices. Rice growing districts like Bilaspur and Raipur in the Chhattisgarh Division of the Central Provinces have no winter crops to speak of, and no alleviation in their condition through the spring harvest could be expected. In Ganjam and Vizagapatam in the Madras Presidency rice is likewise the staple crop, and here also the distressed tracts went from bad to worse. In the Bombay and Madras Deccan the late crops failed in most places, and their harvesting had no effect on prices or on the general condition of the people.

48. The growth of relief from the commencement of relief operations to the end of April 1897 is shown in the table below :—

Provinces.	NUMBER OF PERSONS IN RECEIPT OF RELIEF AT THE END OF EACH MONTH.						
	October 1896.	November 1896.	December 1896.	January 1897.	February 1897.	March 1897.	April 1897.
Madras	—	28,410	26,330	42,363	65,835	104,955	231,650
Bombay	—	10,409	239,356	325,695	412,259	454,443	403,818
Bengal	—	3,384	91,410	338,810	410,002	535,333	678,972
North-Western Provinces and Oudh.	40,880	145,697	496,875	1,254,108	1,647,529	1,010,616	1,248,496
Punjab	5,902	10,919	53,073	97,259	123,738	102,474	87,971
Central Provinces ...	—	—	167,189	284,287	351,263	475,644	581,963
Burma	2,998	20,337	30,134	33,230	26,128	23,605	16,728
Berar	—	—	—	—	11,111	15,627	23,160
Total ..	49,780	219,156	1,104,367	2,375,752	3,047,865	2,722,697	3,272,758
Native States.							
Hyderabad	—	—	—	—	4,509	4,414	26,843
Central India	15,969	Not reported.	30,876	69,062	137,040	100,246	149,596
Rajputana	8,019	34,807	47,254	25,041	19,469	29,808	21,690
Total ...	23,988	34,807	78,130	94,103	161,018	134,468	198,129
GRAND TOTAL ...	73,768	253,963	1,182,497	2,469,855	3,208,883	2,857,168	3,470,887

On the 30th April there were 3,272,758 persons in receipt of relief in British India and 198,129 persons in receipt of relief in Native States. The greatest number attained in any province during this period was 1,647,000 persons in the North-Western Provinces and Oudh at the end of February. In the middle of March the spring harvest in those provinces afforded employment in the fields and withdrew labourers from the relief works. In the Bundelkhand districts of the same provinces the ripening of the flower of the *mahua* tree (*Bassia latifolia*), which in a dried state is very largely used as an article of food throughout Central India, gave further employment to the people, and brought a supply of cheap food within their reach. All this tended to relieve the pressure on the relief works during March and accounts for the fall in the numbers on relief in the North-Western Provinces and Oudh at the close of the month. In April they again began to rise. The effect of the spring harvest in the Punjab is seen in the drop in the April numbers, the harvest there being later. In Bombay the fall in April was due to greater strictness in enforcing tests of distress, especially in the matter of allowances to non-working children. In other provinces the growth of relief is continuous throughout the period, and any tendency which the spring harvest had to draw labour off the relief works was more than counterbalanced by the extension of relief into new areas as the area of distress widened.

Analysis of relief at end of April.

49. As relief varies in character according to the circumstances and physical powers of persons relieved, an analysis of the aggregate volume of relief given on the last day of April is of interest. This is effected by the figures below :—

Provinces.	EMPLOYED ON RELIEF WORKS.			Employed on test works.	Total employed on works.	GRATUITOUSLY RELIEVED.			GRAND TOTAL.
	Workers.	Dependants.	Total.			In poorhouses or kitchens.	In their homes.	Total.	
Madras	184,207	10,266	194,473	7,202	201,675	4,267	25,708	29,975	231,650
Bombay	292,752	79,477	372,229	973	373,202	434	30,182	30,616	403,818
Bengal	345,037	31,998	377,035	9,513	386,548	3,244	289,180	292,424	678,972
North-Western Provinces and Oudh.	781,843	145,588	927,431	7,455	934,886	26,819	286,791	313,610	1,248,496
Punjab	60,684	14,247	74,931	116	75,047	1,666	11,258	12,924	87,971
Central Provinces ...	405,290	75,952	481,242	—	481,242	21,258	79,463	100,721	581,963
Burma	13,320	—	13,320	—	13,320	—	3,408	3,408	16,728
Berar	20,265	—	20,265	—	20,265	—	2,895	2,895	23,160
Total	2,103,398	357,528	2,460,926	25,259	2,486,185	57,688	728,885	786,573	3,272,758
Native States.									
Hyderabad	23,844	—	23,844	—	23,844	—	2,999	2,999	26,843
Central India ...	132,018	—	132,018	—	132,018	—	17,578	17,578	149,596
Rajputana	14,546	—	14,546	—	14,546	—	7,144	7,144	21,690
Total	170,408	—	170,408	—	170,408	—	27,721	27,721	198,129
GRAND TOTAL ...	2,273,806	357,528	2,631,334	25,259	2,656,593	57,688	756,606	814,294	3,470,887

Gratuitous relief in the homes of the people.

50. From these figures it will be seen that more than three-fourths of the persons relieved were employed on public works, the remainder being shown as gratuitously relieved. Labour for all who can do a reasonable amount of work, and gratuitous relief, as far as possible in their villages, for persons incapable of labour, constitute the two main divisions of famine relief. For wanderers and professional beggars poorhouses are provided, but except in the North-Western Provinces and Oudh and the Central Provinces the number of persons so relieved was very small. Gratuitous relief in villages was given most extensively in the two provinces of Bengal and the North-Western Provinces and Oudh, and in Bengal the number of

persons so relieved bore a very high proportion to the number on works. In other provinces up to the end of April this form of relief was sparingly resorted to. In the next period of the famine a very marked change in this respect will be seen in the Central Provinces. No subject during the late famine has been more continuously under observation and discussion than the proper limits of this system of "outdoor" relief in the homes of the people, and it undoubtedly constitutes one of the most difficult and delicate questions in famine administration. A few remarks on the point may therefore not be out of place. The Famine Commission show that in the earlier famines the obligation of relieving persons other than the able-bodied was not recognised by the State, and was considered to rest with the charitable public. The first step to the recognition of the responsibility of the State in this respect was by the institution of poor-houses or kitchens where relief was given in the form of cooked food, with or without the condition of residence. The next step was taken in the Behar famine of 1873-74, when village inspection and village relief were prominent features of Sir Richard Temple's organization. The country was mapped out into small circles, each superintended by a relieving officer, and it was made his duty to discover within his circle all cases of distress which could not be met by the offer of employment on works, and to arrange for the weekly or monthly distribution to such persons of doles of grain or money, availing himself, so far as was possible, of the services of the village headman. The Famine Commission clearly recognised that under this system where no test of distress can be applied the difficulty of distinguishing the worthy from the unworthy must be great. But they noted the fact that the poor-house system was regarded by the people with extreme repulsion, and that it involved the uprooting of families from their homes and the breaking up of social bonds. The Famine Commission accordingly came to the conclusion that the village system was preferable for general adoption "insomuch as, while this system may "involve the risk of a too free grant of relief, the poor-house system involves the "more serious risk of insufficient relief." To it they looked for the prevention of the wandering of the poor in famine time, "which leads to the dissolution of the "village communities, and is one of the principal causes of famine mortality." They thought that if work on the task system commensurate with the capacity of each labourer was offered to all persons capable of doing a reasonable amount of work, the incapable poor who would be supplied with food in their homes would not form a large percentage of the population; and they believed that by means of a complete chain of inspectors in each local area with a European officer at their head abuses could be prevented. The system of gratuitous relief approved by the Famine Commission has been introduced into the Famine Codes, but the present is the first occasion since they were framed on which it has been extensively applied. In the Behar districts of Bengal the percentage of persons gratuitously relieved in their homes was as high as 5 and 6 per cent. of the total population of the distressed tracts. In the North-Western Provinces and Oudh the proportion has exceeded 3 per cent. in three or four districts only, while in many districts it was less than 1 per cent. In either province special pains have been taken to make the supervision efficient and to confine relief to deserving cases, and in either province the local Government is satisfied that it has been the means of keeping together the village and family organization and in preventing wandering and mortality. The intensity of the famine in parts of the North-Western Provinces and Oudh was such that gratuitous relief in the homes of the people on a large scale was inevitable. But the Bengal figures gave cause to inquiries on the part of the Government of India. The local Government has explained them by reference to the chronic poverty of the dense population of Behar and to the rapid drying up of the springs of private charity as a consequence of this poverty on the first approach of hard times. The great preponderance given in Bengal to gratuitous relief still, however, remains singular and as yet not fully explained. It may be the case that necessitous cases were more completely tracked out in Behar by the very strong relief establishments entertained there, than was possible in other provinces where the staff was weaker and the area of distress more extensive. It is also probable that the strictness with which tasks have been enforced on the relief works in Behar indirectly resulted in a comparatively large number of persons being placed on gratuitous relief, since they were found unable to perform what was held to be a reasonable amount of work. In other provinces where less attention was paid to the amount of work obtained from the relief workers, persons were admitted to the works whose labour was of a nominal character, while the number of women and children among the workers was much in excess of what was required or could be profitably employed. This was in accordance with the principle that it is better to accept all inefficient labourers offering themselves than to place them on gratuitous relief in their homes. Though the labour they are capable of may be of little or no value, they submit, it is held, to a distinct test of distress in the very act of appearing on a relief work. In Bengal inefficient labourers were in principle admitted to the relief works, and the local Government after inquiry came to the conclusion that the gratuitous lists contained the names of no persons who were capable of labour. But there is little doubt that inefficient labourers were in smaller proportion on relief works in Bengal than elsewhere. This appears both from the comparatively few women and children on relief works in Bengal, and from the high tasks which were obtained from the gangs. A difference of system in the management of relief works is indicated, which on the face of it had something to do with the large numbers in Behar on gratuitous relief in their homes. Such divergencies in the methods of relief administration in the different provinces do not necessarily imply that one province has been right and the other wrong. The cause may lie in the special circumstances of the case. In Behar the relief works were small and numerous and within easy reach of every village. If great attention had not been paid to exacting a high task from the labourers and thus indirectly eliminating inefficient persons, the works would have attracted unmanageable crowds, and this might have been a greater danger than some excess in the matter of gratuitous relief. It may also be mentioned in noticing the high percentage of gratuitous relief in the homes of the people in Behar that in other provinces more gratuitous relief on the relief works themselves was given than was the case in Behar. Under what conditions and to what classes this second form of gratuitous relief is given will be explained later on when the system of relief works is discussed.

51. In the Central Provinces the scattered and sparse population, the migratory habits of the aboriginal races, the defective communications, and the weakness of the establishments at the disposal of the administration, made the effective organisation of village relief peculiarly arduous. Pending its completion the expedient of "relief centres," where food was supplied to all comers in obvious need of relief, was provisionally adopted. To these relief centres was often attached a small relief work, such as the excavation of a village tank or the repairing of a road, and when this was the case able-bodied applicants for relief were required to perform a task as the condition of relief. These centres proved very useful in the wilder tracts, and as a simple and summary method of relief they were frequently resorted to in places where distress unexpectedly made its appearance before regular relief works could be opened. But they tended to become unmanageable as the applicants for relief increased, and were gradually discarded, except in the wilder tracts, as relief operations were systematised. Both in poor-houses and in relief centres in the Central Provinces the mortality was very high in the early months of the famine and attracted public attention. The death statistics of these institutions collated by the local Administration show that a large proportion of the deaths were those of wanderers from native territory or other parts of India. This was especially the case in the Nerbadda valley districts which form the natural channel of communication between Central India and the fertile south, and which in all seasons are resorted to for work and food by thousands of immigrants from the north. But many of the deaths were those of aborigines or of residents of other districts of the province, indicating the prevalence of wandering to a lamentable extent. This aimless wandering of hunger-stricken persons has often characterised great famines in the past, and however vigilant the administration, it is likely to occur in broken forest country among people who largely subsist on wild fruits and grasses and who still retain the nomad's instinct. Many of the difficulties which have arisen in the Central Provinces in the late famine can be traced to this source.

In Madras and Bombay during this period the administration of poor-houses and gratuitous relief in villages presents no features of special interest.

Gratuitous relief to "dependants"

52. Turning now to the main branch of famine relief—the relief works—the gratuitous relief given in connection with them may in the first place be noticed. The wage earned by a relief-worker is not intended to be more than a subsistence

wage. If therefore the people come in families to the relief works, there will be a certain number of children below the working age, and of infirm adults, to be provided for. The Famine Codes allow these non-workers to be gratuitously relieved as "dependants" of the relief-workers, the relief taking the form of money or cooked food. The proportion of dependants to the workers varied greatly, as will be seen from the analysis of the population on relief at the end of April, in different provinces. It was 18 per cent. in the North-Western Provinces and Oudh, and 26 per cent. in Bombay. In Bengal and Madras it was only 9 per cent. and 5 per cent. respectively. These variations were due to the relative extent to which in each province the relief-work population resided on the works; and the practice of residence again depended on the distance of the works from the homes of the people, and on the degree to which residence on them was encouraged, or was enforced as a test of distress. In the North-Western Provinces and in Bombay large works at considerable intervals were the rule, and residence on them was practically obligatory for the majority of the workers, coming as they did from long distances. Whole families settled down on the works, and the non-working members had to be gratuitously relieved. In Bengal the works were so numerous and scattered that there was very little residence on them. The workers came from and returned to their villages daily, and their wives and children, if entitled to gratuitous relief, were relieved in their homes, and not as "dependants" on the works. The same was the case in Madras.

53. To the relief worker the gratuitous relief of his "dependants" is very attractive, especially when it takes the form of cash. In Bombay the large number of non-working children brought by women to the works in the first months of the scarcity led to inquiry which resulted in the discovery that many of the children belonged to persons who did not attend the works and that they were lent for the occasion. This practice was stopped by the institution of children's kitchens in connection with the works and the discontinuance of the money dole. Elsewhere a similar change was necessitated by the neglect of parents to feed their children, though receiving money for their food. It was found that they either spent the extra allowance on themselves, or saved it against the day when the works would be closed. Famine weakens family affections, and there is no clearer sign of its severity in a given locality than the condition of the children. Wherever children's kitchens were substituted for cash allowances an immediate improvement in the health of the children ensued. The experience of the late famine is conclusive on the point that when distress becomes severe, parents cannot be trusted to provide for their offspring.

54. This fact constitutes one of the arguments in favour of the retention of the present relief wage system of the Famine Codes, demoralizing though it may seem in some of its aspects. Under this system the relief worker, whatever may be his working capacity, is restricted to a bare subsistence wage. The extra allowances receivable by him for non-working members of his family depend not on his industry but on the size of the family. The alternative system, which is not without its advocates, is to permit the worker to earn enough by exceptional industry to support himself and the persons dependent upon him. It is easy to see that this would result in the State paying many of the workers more than they actually require for their own subsistence, without any guarantee that the young, the aged and infirm would be kept alive. When distress is slight this consideration has not the same force, and if sufficient wages are offered to the people the care of their dependants may be left to the able-bodied as in ordinary times. In slightly affected areas during the late famine several varieties of the piece-work system, under which the worker is permitted, in proportion to his industry and skill, to earn a wage in excess of a bare subsistence for himself and receives no separate allowance for his dependants, were tried with success.

The organization of relief works.

55. The first period of the famine was occupied in all provinces with the organization of relief works, and in connection with this the disposition of famine labour to the best advantage received much attention. Such disposition includes (*a*) the selection of suitable works of permanent public utility; (*b*) the management of the works by a competent staff; (*c*) the proper classification and remuneration of the relief workers; (*d*) the proper tasking of the workers; (*e*) the adoption of other self-acting tests of distress.

56. The selection of suitable works for the employment of relief workers is a matter of greater difficulty than it at first sight seems. Under the ideal system there should be in every distressed area one or more projects of permament utility, specially prepared and reserved for the emergency of a famine. Such projects should be capable of giving employment to a large body of labourers for several months, and as the labour is unskilled, they should preferentially consist of earthwork or of quarrying and preparing metal for roads. Railway earthwork, canal and drainage excavation, road-making and road-repairs, and tank construction almost exhaust the category of such possible works. But there are many districts for which no new railways are proposed, in which no canal can be made, and where tanks of large size for irrigation purposes are not required. In such cases road earthwork and the collection of metal are usually the one form of labour on which the relief population can be employed, and the quantity of such work that can usefully be undertaken is necessarily limited. The Punjab was fortunate in having two canal projects (the Ghaggar canal in the Hissar district and the Jhelum canal in the Gujrat district) ready for immediate execution in the distressed tracts, besides the earthwork for several branch railways. In Upper Burma canal projects were also available. In Bombay the collection of road-metal was first resorted to, but when it was seen that a supply sufficient to last for years was being accumulated, several large tank projects for irrigation purposes and railway earthwork were commenced. In Madras there was a singular scarcity of large projects of permanent utility, and the relief gangs have been employed on road repairs and the collection of road metal. In the Central Provinces the earthwork of the Raipur-Dhamtari railway gave some employment in the Raipur district, and that of the Katni-Saugor railway in the Saugor district ; but road-work here also has been the chief resource. In the North-Western Provinces and Oudh also road-work has been the chief form of employment, and in the worst districts every existing unmetalled road has been put into thorough repair and often raised and widened, and many new roads constructed. Village and road side tanks within a certain distance from each road so operated upon were also deepened and improved as part of the road project. In the North-Western Provinces and Oudh and to a lesser extent in the Central Provinces the road-works, which were almost invariably large works giving employment in each case to 2,000 workers and upwards, were supplemented by numerous small works, such as village roads and tanks, for the employment of small bodies of labourers. The difficulty of effective supervision over such scattered works was recognised, and to meet it the aid of the local landowners was called in. They would agree to construct a given village work for a certain sum, covenanting to employ distressed persons only and to pay them famine wages. In some cases the cost was shared between the landowner and the Government, in others the Government bore the whole cost. But in either case the landowner had a strong pecuniary interest in getting a full day's work out of the labourers. No return of the village works constructed through this agency has yet been received, but they are known to have been numerous, especially in the Allahabad Division of the North-Western Provinces and in the Chhattisgarh Division of the Central Provinces, where the country lends itself to the construction of small tanks for the storage of water. As subsidiary to large works under direct State management these "village works" have proved very useful, but neither in the Central Provinces nor in the North-Western Provinces has it been found safe to trust to them alone. A backbone of large works on which labourers can be employed in thousands under strict professional supervision and control was held in both provinces to be essential. In Bengal there were no large projects ready in the first months of the famine, and, owing to the character of the country, tanks were preferred in Behar to road-making. A few of the tank projects were large, but the majority were virtually "village works." And, being comparatively small, the works opened in each district were necessarily very numerous. Effective supervision would not have been possible had not the special famine establishments in Behar been exceptionally strong.

(a.) The works selected.

57. From what has been said above, it will be understood that there is less to show in the way of permanent public utility for the enormous quantity of famine

relief labour which has been employed by the State than could be wished. This is more or less inevitable whenever labour is employed for reasons other than because it is wanted. But more attention may usefully be directed in future by local Governments to the preparation of famine-relief projects, especially in provinces where during the late famine difficulty has been experienced in providing large works of undeniable utility.

(*b*.) The controlling staff.

Except in Bengal, where, owing to the numerical weakness of the Public Works Department it was found necessary at first to place almost all relief works under the civil officers, the immediate direction of the larger relief works was from the outset entrusted to officers of the Public Works Department. But as such works are carried on on the principle of giving effectual relief to the labouring population and not of getting the greatest quantity of work done at the cheapest rate, civil officers were associated with the officers of the Public Works Department to see that the labourers were correctly classified and properly paid and tasked according to their strength. In such a system of dual control there is obviously room for discussion as to the limits of the respective powers of the civil and professional authorities unless they are clearly defined beforehand. The Famine Codes have been found to be wanting in precision in this respect, though fortunately in most provinces this has not been productive of many difficulties. In Madras a certain amount of friction appears to have arisen, and the professional officers would seem to have been subordinated to the civil authorities to a greater extent than elsewhere. The question chiefly arises as regards the regulation of tasks and the imposition of fines for short work. Viewed in the light of results the Madras practice compared unfavourably with that of other provinces where greater powers in all that appertains to the technical management of relief works were given to the Department of Public Works.

(*c*.) The classification and wages of the workers.

58. The classification and wages of the relief workers are prescribed in much detail by rules in the Famine Codes which elaborate the principle laid down by the Famine Commission that to all who can do a reasonable amount of work shall be given "a task carefully adjusted to their powers" and "a wage on which life and health can be maintained." These rules are in the main based on the experience gained in recent scarcities. But they had not been tested on a large scale, and the test to which this year they have been subjected has shown that they are capable of improvement. In some respects their provisions are imperfect and in others greater flexibility of system is desirable to suit the very diverse conditions which the famine administrator has to meet. The first in the field in the matter was the Government of the North-Western Provinces and Oudh. Profiting by its experience in the previous year in Bundelkhand that Government supplemented its Famine Code by a large body of instructions which appear to have worked well, and which in substance were adopted in Bengal and the Central Provinces. In the classification of the relief-workers and the wage-scale some important changes were made. The Famine Codes recognise four classes of labourers—the professional digger or navvy, the able-bodied worker who is not a professional but who is accustomed to hard manual labour, the able-bodied person who is not accustomed to manual labour, and the weakly person. It is contemplated that these four classes of workers should do tasks graduated according to their respective capacities, and be paid according to a graduated wage scale. In this scale the wage for each class is a ration of so many ounces of flour and pulse, with a little salt and condiments, converted into cash according to the market price of the ration. At the bottom of the scale is the wage of the weakly person whose employment is presumably nominal, and who is presumed to require less food than the able-bodied workers. The wages of the other three classes are built up from this minimum wage. The Government of the North-Western Provinces and Oudh in its instructions simplified this classification. As the relief workers are ordinarily employed on earthwork of the simplest kind, needing only two classes of labourers—the digger and the carrier—the instructions recognised two classes of workers only, and two rates of wage. The carriers who formed the great mass of the workers and who were chiefly women and children, received a wage which was practically the minimum wage of the Code. The digger received a somewhat

higher wage. When the price of grain was Re. 1 for 10 seers, the digger's wage was 1¾ annas and the adult carrier's 1¼ annas. The child over 12 received 1 anna and the child between 7 and 12 half an anna. Under this system the average remuneration of the famine labourers was less than what it would have been under the Code. But it seems to have been found sufficient to keep the workers in good health. For Sundays they received a holiday wage, and additional allowances for the non-working members of the family. In this way the aggregate wages of a family of five persons possibly amounted to Rs. 8 or Rs. 10 a month. With food at normal prices this would be riches to an Indian villager: and even with food at famine prices it is said to have allowed a small margin for saving.

59. While the wage-scale of the Code was considered in Upper India to be if any thing too liberal, it was found fault with in Madras for being too low. Influenced by the reports of its Sanitary Commissioner on the condition of the relief work population, the Government of Madras represented to the Government of India that the lower grades of the wage scale were insufficient to maintain workers in good health. Into the details of the discussion it is unnecessary to go. The view taken by the Government of India was that the scale had been found sufficient in other provinces, especially in Bombay where the conditions of life were very similar, and that a case for raising it and thereby augmenting the already very heavy expenditure on famine relief was not made out to their satisfaction. The Government of Madras acquiesced in this conclusion and the matter dropped.

60. Thus the final word on the question of the famine wage and the classification of famine workers has yet to be spoken. When the Provincial Governments come to review the famine operations in which they have been engaged and to consider the bearing of the experience so acquired on the Famine Codes, this question among others will engage attention. The reports of the officer deputed by the Government of India to inspect the relief works in all the provinces deal fully with it and will greatly assist to its solution. It may possibly be that no absolute wage standard, which is under all circumstances sufficient for the worker's support and not more than sufficient, can be laid down. A wage that is sufficient in a slightly distressed tract or at the commencement of a scarcity, when the workers have still some resources of their own, and when there is a risk of withdrawing them unnecessarily from their ordinary employments, may be insufficient during acute distress, or in the late stage of famine. It is a primary principle that at no time should the wage be such as to attract labour which otherwise could support itself. And when this happens, the wage has to be reduced below even the theoretical bare subsistence allowance, or else the other conditions of the relief, such as the amount of the task or the Sunday dole or the allowances for "dependants" have to be modified.

(*d.*) **The tasking of the workers.**

61. The proper tasking of the workers is, to quote the Famine Commissioners, required "to prevent the relief work "from being so light or unduly attractive as "to induce any to remain who are not really in want." To this matter much attention has been directed, especially in the first period of the famine. The system at first adopted in the North-Western Provinces and Oudh was to group the relief-workers into gangs of 60 or 80, of whom about one-fourth were able-bodied diggers and the rest carriers, and to fix a daily task (of so many cubic feet of earth dug and carried) for the gang. As the carriers were usually in excess of the number actually required, any deficiency in work was the fault of the diggers. This led to the rule that if the work of the gang was short, the diggers and the diggers only were fined. As experience was gained in the management of large bodies of relief-workers and the supervising establishments became more expert, it was found possible in place of dealing with the gang as a unit to mark out the day's task for each digger, and to enforce its performance on each individual. In Bengal a smaller unit than the gang of 80 was adopted, but in other respects the system of tasking resembled that in force in the North-Western Provinces and Oudh. In all provinces the enforcement of a reasonable labour task was found to be hampered by two circumstances peculiar to the employment of famine relief-workers. The first is that the number of women and children and other inefficient workers seeking employment is usually much in excess of the efficient

male workers. In the North-Western Provinces and Oudh there were in April only 32 male adults in every hundred workers; in Bombay 31, and in Madras 27. In Bengal the ratio was much higher, the male adult workers being 46 per cent. of the whole. Now, if the work on which the relief population is placed consists of road-making or tank-excavation or other form of earthwork, inefficient labour can be employed in considerable quantities, but there is a point beyond which room cannot be profitably found for it. When the point is reached, the famine administrator has to be content with a nominal task from labourers of this class, and must confine himself to fully tasking the efficient minority of workers. The second difficulty lies in the necessity of keeping the relief-population, whatever be the result of their labour, in fairly good health, and this can only be attained by paying each person a wage sufficient for his or her bare subsistence. As the full famine wage earnable by a worker who completes his allotted task is little, if anything, above a bare subsistence wage, the power of the officer in charge of the works to fine for short work is necessarily very limited. When this fact is realised by the workers, the temptation to idle is considerable, especially if they are unaccustomed to regular spade-work and the task is such that it can only be accomplished by strenuous exertion. The task therefore has to be essentially moderate, and in adapting it to the average working capacity of the people and in getting it done by them without frequent resort to fining and without deterring weak or inefficient workers a good deal of care and management on the part of the directing staff is required. The progress made in these respects as relief operations progressed appears to have been very marked in most provinces. In the North-Western Provinces and Oudh, although the inefficient labour was in large excess and low tasks the rule, the amount of work obtained from the workers improved month by month. In the Punjab where the relief-workers were exceptionally able-bodied and expert, the standard of work on the Ghaggar and Jhelum canals fell little below the ordinary standard for non-famine labour. In Behar, where great attention from the first was paid to the subject and where the proportion of inefficient labour was never excessive, a high task was enforced for months. In Bombay and in the Central Provinces the task imposed has, as a rule, been fully sufficient to constitute a real test of distress. This was also the case in Madras at the beginning of the period, but in April the Madras Government were led by considerations regarding the heat of the season, the distances which the workers had daily to travel to the works from their homes, and the reported weakness of some of the gangs, to authorise reductions in the tasks. These reductions appear to have been injudiciously granted in not a few cases by the subordinate officials; they conferred on the relief works an undesirable degree of popularity and greatly augmented the number of the workers, and they eventually were recognised to be excessive and demoralising, and were withdrawn or curtailed.

(*e*) Other tests.

62. The obvious drawbacks which in spite of the best management attend the task and subsistence wage system of the Famine Codes have led to several experiments of great interest and value. The problem was how to safely reduce the excessive numbers of inefficient workers, and to infuse more energy and industry into the able-bodied minority. It was at once recognised, as indeed the Famine Commissioners had pointed out, that ordinary piecework, under which only "remunerative" labour is employed and is paid by results, would not be suitable. If the rate of payment were adjusted to meet the powers of the least capable persons seeking employment, the work would be made enormously costly; and if it were not so adjusted, relief would be virtually denied to large classes in urgent need of it. But it was thought that if work were given out to family groups or other small parties of workers, if a fair wage were allowed according as a higher or a lower task was performed by the group, and if its earnings were restricted to a maximum sum a day, the chief objections to ordinary piece-work would be obviated, and the relief requirements of tracts where distress was not severe would be sufficiently and economically met. It is unnecessary here to describe the experiments made on these lines in the North-Western Provinces, Bengal and the Central Provinces. But it may be said that in districts not acutely distressed they have proved successful. The number of inefficient workers has thereby been largely reduced, and relief attended with much economy. Where each individual worker receives a subsistence wage, however little be works, and when every

"dependant" incapable of labour is also supported, it is the interest of the head of every household to bring all members of it upon the relief-works. When, however, in place of these conditions work is paid for according to results, and the workers are expected to maintain their children and their aged relatives, the attendance at the works is at once reduced. In the projected revision of the Famine Codes this system of petty piece-work or modified task-work will probably find a place, as an expedient preferable to the strict "task and minimum wage" system of the present codes in cases where distress is not widespread and severe.

63. With upwards of two millions of persons employed on relief works in British India, at the cost of about Rs. 2,00,000 (Rx.* 20,000) a day, the Government of India in February thought it expedient that the principles regulating expenditure on public works in time of famine should be defined and announced to Local Governments. These instructions, which are dated the 13th February 1897, may here be noticed, as they in effect conveyed approval to the experimental departures from the relief system of the Famine Codes which have just been described. The instructions open by setting out the general rule that in tracts where no distress exists, expenditure upon public works, even within the limits of budget provision, should be contracted with a view to setting funds and establishments at liberty for employment where they are more needed. To this rule exceptions are recognized where work cannot be contracted without risk of creating distress by reducing local employment of labour, or of returning to districts where distress exists or is threatening the labourers employed on them. In districts where distress exists and additional employment has to be provided, all expenditure on such object must be subject to certain relief conditions. The primary condition is that the remuneration for work done should be so fixed as not to attract labour for which employment exists elsewhere. The method of enforcing this condition will, however, vary with the degree of distress. Where distress is acute, and employment has to be provided not only for able-bodied labourers but also for a large proportion of inefficient labour, the rigorous enforcement of task-work is necessary, nobody being allowed to do more than the fixed task or to earn more than the minimum wage. In this way alone can the supply of useful work on which labour can be employed be economised, and expenditure be limited. Where distress is less acute, and the proportion of inefficient labour seeking employment is not great, payment by results, it was said, is more economical than task-work; for so long as an able-bodied labourer can earn enough to enable those of his family who ordinarily do not work to remain at home, he will support himself and them more cheaply than the Government can. When payment by results is adopted, the rates offered should be so regulated as not to attract labour from existing employments elsewhere. If the demand by inefficient labour for employment should increase when the payment-by-result system is in force, it should be first met by opening test-works under ordinary task conditions; and if it should continuously increase, the existence of acute distress might be assumed, and thereupon "payment by results must be discontinued and task-work substituted for it." These instructions have, it is believed, been found to be in general conformity with the additional experience acquired since they were issued, and they summarise by anticipation the results of the experiments in the employment of relief-labour which have been under trial in different provinces, and which will be fully reported on in the near future by the local Governments.

The Government and the Grain Trade. The rule of non-intervention.

64. In the earlier part of this narrative the rapidity with which prices of all food-grains rose to famine rates in the autumn of 1896, and the apprehensions felt in Bengal and the Central Provinces that supplies might locally fail in special localities, have been noticed. It was inevitable that the position of the Government with regard to the provision of food for the population generally, for the people collected on relief works, and for particular tracts where from one cause or another failure of local stocks was anticipated, should come under consideration and discussion. It has been stated that in November the Government of Bengal, in commenting on the report of the Commis-

* Rx. stands for tens of rupees, or "rupee-pounds."

sioner of the Patna Division and in showing that it implied a deficiency of 550,000 tons in the available food-supply of Behar for the year, touched on the question whether private trade could be relied on to supply the deficiency. "The "high prices in Eastern Bengal and the indications of distress already "existing in districts that were always considered free from scarcity "show," wrote the Bengal Government, "that little reliance can be placed "on supplies from within the province." The importation of wheat from abroad, and of rice from Burma, seemed possible, and the Government of Bengal was disposed to hope, though not without some misgivings, that the food wants of the province would be met by private trade. This belief was very decidedly held by the Government of India. But the idea of the Government entering the market as a purchaser appears to have gained currency with the public, as during the month several overtures were received from mercantile houses to purchase grain on behalf of the Government in Burma and America. To all these the reply was given that the Government had no intention of making purchases on its own account or of in any way interfering with the general course of trade. In December the Government of Bengal became aware that many gentlemen of position and local knowledge in Behar considered that stocks, especially in the less accessible places, were likely to be depleted before private trade could supply the local deficit, and applied to the Government of India to authorise advances of money being made to traders and other persons in Behar for the purchase and import of foreign food-grains. The Government of Bengal in making the proposal was disposed to think that it would not constitute an interference with private trade. The Government of India thought otherwise. They regarded the scheme as one for the importation of food-grains from abroad into India with funds to be supplied by Government. As such they felt obliged to negative it. This they did in a letter of the 4th January 1897, which, as a declaration of policy and a contradiction of the rumours afloat as to the action of the Government, was published in the *Gazette of India* for general information. In this letter the Government of India recognised the grave possibility that in certain circumstances the food-supply of the country taken as a whole might prove insufficient, and that it might require to be supplemented by importations from abroad. But they held that even in that event the best policy was that of rigid abstention from interference with the machinery of mercantile trade. They believed that, although the State might do more than one trader, it would certainly do less than the trade. "The Governor-General in Council," they said, "believes that the intervention of Government "as a purchaser or importer would do infinitely more harm than good, as it would "cripple and discourage the agency which is best able to gauge the need, which is "impelled by self-interest to anticipate it, and which alone is best able to supply "it effectively." The functions of Government in the matter should, it was explained, be confined to assisting the trade with information, guaranteeing by means of its relief system that the demand of the public for food shall be an effective demand, and giving every possible facility for the free movement and distribution of grain. The exceptions to the general policy of non-interference suggested by the Famine Commissioners were then discussed and shown to be confined to two cases, the case of assisting trade to provide supplies on a relief work, and of assisting or supplementing trade in remote or inaccessible tracts. Interference in Behar, they considered, should, if permitted at all, be strictly confined to these two classes of cases and to particular and well defined localities. In reply to this letter the Government of Bengal explained that it had always intended to strictly confine its action to tracts where special local circumstances made intervention necessary, and that on the general question of principle its views were identical with those of the Imperial Government. So far as the Government of Bengal was concerned the discussion here closed, a general permission being accorded to the local Government to make such arrangements in these special tracts as were considered necessary, without further reference to the Government of India. But the general declaration of policy unquestionably had a re-assuring effect on trade. The level of prices in India and abroad was against an active import of American grain, and losses are said to have been made over cargoes of wheat. But Burma had a large surplus of rice, and rice imports grew to large dimensions. In Behar the up-country dealers gained confidence and steadily extended their operations, and aided by the excellent railway system which links the province with the rest of India they succeeded in making good the deficiencies of local stocks without assistance from the Government. The net imports of food-grains into Behar from November 1896 to the end of August 1897 are returned at 120,000 tons, a figure substantially below the half million tons which at one time would, it was thought, be needed. As regards Behar, therefore, the success of the policy of non-intervention was unquestionable.

Intervention in exceptional cases.

65. In Bengal, the only case in which intervention was considered necessary was that of the Palamau District in the Division of Chota Nagpur. The distance of this district from the railway and large grain marts, the inertness of trade, and the exhaustion of local stocks created a situation which was regarded as serious by the local authorities. Accordingly the Government of Bengal with the concurrence of the Government of India gave a small bounty on all grain imported into the district before the 1st April. The period was subsequently extended to the end of June. As this measure was found insufficient, the Government in July imported 500 tons of Burma rice on its own account. In the Central Provinces the isolated condition of the Mandla District situated on the Satpura plateau gave cause for anxiety. Local stocks were reported to be exhausted and the grain trade was confined to small dealers. The district is remote from the railway, the communications even in the open season are rough and difficult, and are liable to be closed for days together by heavy rain. It was therefore deemed prudent before the setting in of the rainy season to give contracts for the supply of some of the relief camps to outside grain merchants, to undertake direct importation for other camps, and to give advances to local traders for relief centres and bazaars. These measures proved sufficient. Similar anxiety was also felt about the contiguous Baihar sub-division of the Balaghat district, but eventually it was found that private trade was sufficiently active and resourceful and that intervention was not necessary. In this and other localities, however, in the Central Provinces special measures for the importation of seed-grain were taken, as it was found that local stocks had run out, and that particular kinds of seed-grain were required and could only be procured from a distance. In these cases the Government officers in importing the grain made arrangements to place it in store with responsible landowners against the advent of the rains, when it was advanced to cultivators for sowing, either on behalf of the State or of the Indian Charitable Relief Fund.

66. These instances indicate the very limited extent to which it was found necessary to interfere with or to supplement the ordinary operations of the grain-trade. At the same time material aid was given to traders by the railways, which with a view of encouraging import of grain from the ports reduced their upward rates to a level with their seaward rates. In Bombay, Madras, and the North-Western Provinces and Oudh the trade seems from the outset to have proved fully equal to all calls made upon it. Even the provisioning of the large relief camps, where bodies of 5,000 or 6,000 persons were collected, gave rise to no difficulty. There was frequently very keen competition for permission to act as purveyors of the camps, and the activity of the trade induced many persons with petty capital to turn to grain-dealing and temporarily to join the ranks of the professionals. Wherever there was a railway, grain freely moved along its length at the least movement of prices. The district of Allahabad from January to May imported by rail an average of 1,800 tons of grain a week, representing the food-supply of half a million persons. The Banda district in the same period imported 600 tons a week. The weekly import into the Poona district averaged 900 tons, and into the Hissar district 1,000 tons. Grain came from long distances and was dropped down at little way-side stations which have never before seen such traffic. From January to the end of April the despatches of grain, chiefly Burma rice, from Calcutta to stations in the North-Western Provinces and Oudh amounted to 77,000 tons. Burma rice found its way first to relief camps and then into the village bazaars throughout the country. All this was accomplished by the ordinary machinery of commerce, encouraged by low railway rates, an effective demand for food, and the complete abstention of the State from interference of any kind.

67. Among native States the first instinct was to resort to the traditional expedient of prohibiting export of grain. It is a measure very popular with the official classes, the poorer members of which are considerably affected by a rise in the price of food. In December information reached the Government of India that export to the Bombay Presidency from Indore and from Hyderabad had been prohibited by the respective States, and that similar action was about to be taken by the States of Central India and Rajputana. Political Officers were instructed to explain very fully to the States to which they were attached the reasons why the prohibition or the taxation of exports was held by economists to be mischievous and useless, and to advise reconsideration of the matter. This advice was generally adopted and the restrictions removed. Few, if any, cases occurred in which the local grain supply actually failed in the territories of a Native State during the late famine. In the Bastar State, a rugged and remote tract which occupies the south-east angle of the Central Provinces, apprehensions were felt in January lest the large exports of grain which were taking place from it to the Central Provinces would reduce the stocks to danger point, and the Administrator was authorised, as an alternative to his original wish to prohibit export, to buy up and store a reserve of grain for the people against the rains. But further enquiry showed that there was no ground for apprehension. The harvests had not failed. The cultivators had large stocks in hand, for in ordinary years the distance of Bastar from good markets checks export. They were selling their surplus at much profit to themselves, and the alarm was purely an official one. This is a good illustration of the class of cases which frequently occur when prices rise in India, and exemplifies the necessity for caution in dealing with popular apprehensions that the food supply of a district is running short because the exports happen to be large.

Native States and the grain-trade.

VII.—The third period. From the close of the spring harvest to the establishment of the monsoon rains.

68. The third period opened with the completion of the rabi harvest in Upper India and with the setting in in Southern India, Burma and Bengal of the showers which in those parts precede the regular monsoon rains, and which there enable early rain crops to be sown and lands to be prepared for later sowings. The middle portion of the period was one of great anxiety, as the monsoon, after an early and satisfactory start, died away. The crops which by the third week in June had been sown over large areas were seriously imperilled, and great loss of seed was anticipated. But before the period had closed the monsoon recovered strength, and sufficient rain fell in most provinces to save the crops already sown and to permit sowings to be resumed. The exceptions to this were the Deccan country in Madras and Bombay, the northern districts of Madras, the Punjab and Burma. These areas did not receive sufficient rain until, in the case of the Punjab, the end of August, and in the case of the Deccan, the northern districts of Madras, and Burma, until the middle of September.

Character of the period.

69. In the first half of this period the numbers on relief reached a maximum. During May the rise was especially marked in the North-Western Provinces, Madras, the Central Provinces and Bengal. At the end of May the total number of persons receiving relief in British India and Native States exceeded four millions. This figure was maintained during the second fortnight of June. A sharp decline then took place—chiefly in the North-Western Provinces and Oudh where the rains had opened favourably—and this was maintained till the close of June. At the end of June the total numbers on relief were 3¼ millions. The numbers in Madras showed a large increase on the May figures. In the North-Western Provinces and Oudh they had fallen by nearly one-half, and in the Central Provinces by one-third. In Bombay and Bengal the decrease was less. In the first fortnight of July, owing to the break in the rains, the numbers on relief again rose to 3½ millions, falling however by the end of the month to little over three millions. The increase in the numbers on relief in Madras continued, and on the 31st July that province headed the list with a relief population of 806,000.

Numbers rise in May and June.

Bombay also on that date showed an increase on the May and June figures, though in a very much less degree. The numbers in the North-Western Provinces and Bengal had continued to decline. The Central Provinces showed an increase on the June figures, but a decrease on those for May. The table below gives the numbers on relief in each Province and Native State on the last day of the first and second fortnight of each month of the period :—

Provinces.	Number of Persons in Receipt of Relief at the end of each Fortnight.						
	April.	May.		June.		July.	
	Second-half.	First-half.	Second-half.	First-half.	Second-half.	First-half.	Second-half.
Madras	231,650	285,461	396,413	464,702	620,105	792,891	806,977
Bombay	403,818	377,810	352,034	329.634	317,243	384.912	408,080
Bengal	678,972	782,088	833,447	824,080	719,116	648,778	561,889
North-Western Provinces and Oudh	1,248,496	1,356,162	1.471,123	1,426,266	798.552	766,767	505,476
Punjab	87,971	89,470	96,368	104,850	97,640	60,502	35.910
Central Provinces	581,963	651,576	697,530	659,989	479,972	574,340	602.863
Burma	16,728	14.578	18,277	13,944	22,959	25,600	33,797
Berar	23.160	26.902	30,472	25,051	32,420	33,788	28,929
Total	3,272,758	3,584,047	3,895,654	3,848,516	3,088,007	3,287,578	2,984,821
Native States.							
Hyderabad	26,843	27,472	40,537	28,382	14,063	12,927	17,489
Central India	149,596	176,873	128,454	205,246	123,820	93,694	63,297
Rajputana	21,690	22,515	22,520	24,724	24,593	16,112	10,690
Total	198,129	226,860	191,511	258,352	162.476	122,733	91,476
Grand Total ...	3,470,887	3,810,907	4,087.165	4,106,868	3,250,483	3,410,311	3,076,297

Character of relief in first half of period.

70. The rise and fall in each province were chiefly due to the varying character of the rains and the extent to which they favoured agricultural operations and enabled the population on relief to resume their ordinary occupations. Except in Southern India, Burma and Bengal, where showers in advance of the monsoon give a start to cultivation, the month of May is the idlest period of the Indian agricultural year. Work in the fields is suspended, the harvests have been thrashed and garnered, the sun-burnt earth refuses the plough, and time hangs heavy on the peasant's hands. In this dead season the lack of other employment would in any year bring labourers in almost any district on to a relief work, if one were opened, unless it were managed on very strict conditions. In a year of severe distress and high prices the inclination of the people to flock to relief works in the weeks before the rain has to be reckoned with by the famine administrator, and his plans framed accordingly. His establishments and his programme of works have to be enlarged, and he has to see on the one hand that the widening circle of distress and the deepening of privation are fully met by his measures for relief, and on the other that the offer of relief is not made unduly attractive. He has so to hold the people in hand that the able-bodied among them may be returned in fair health to their fields as soon as the longed for rain descends, and that the weakly and resourceless minority may still be helped along by state relief until they too, as the pressure of want and high prices relaxes, may fall back into their accustomed place in the village economy. These were the guiding principles on which relief measures were shaped in the several provinces in the period now described. In May and the first fortnight of June the crowds on the relief works increased, and the lists of those gratuitously relieved in their homes lengthened. Tasks generally were made more severe, and wages reduced to better test the needs of the workers, while in less distressed districts of Upper India, the modified forms of piece-work which have above been described were

experimentally introduced. To famine-relief officers and their establishments it was a time of extreme tension, of labour under the most trying conditions, and of endless anxieties. In the relief camps water became scarce, and sickness broke out. In the Allahabad district a severe epidemic of cholera led to the dispersal of the large relief camps, and the drafting of the workers in small parties to "village" works, which had been provided beforehand by the local Government for such a contingency. In the Central Provinces cholera was equally destructive in many districts, and the Chief Commissioner had to deplore the loss of some of his best officers. Along with this expansion of relief to meet the immediate necessities of the people, measures were taken to provide the more needy with seed, or with money to buy seed and cattle, against the approaching rainy season. Loans were made for this purpose without interest or at low rates of interest by the State, and over a crore of rupees (Rx. 1,000,000) was placed at the disposal of district committees by the Indian Charitable Famine Relief Fund, to be distributed for this and other objects.

Character of relief in second half of period.

71. With the setting in of the rains in the latter half of June the scheme of relief in Upper and Central India was materially altered. The landless agricultural labourers who formed the bulk of the relief-workers could now find employment in the fields, and it became doubly important to curtail whatever attractions the relief works possessed and to offer no inducements to able-bodied persons to linger on them who could find work elsewhere. This was effectively done in the North-Western Provinces and Oudh by reducing the number of relief works and by substituting some form of piece-work for the code system of task-work, with its attractions of a subsistence wage and allowances for Sundays and dependants. In the third week in June the number of persons on relief works in those Provinces was thus reduced from 953,000 to 433,000. In Bengal the numbers on relief works similarly fell from 410,000 to 298,000. In the Central Provinces from 538,000 to 428,000. The process of reduction would have been still more rapid but for the continued dearness of food and the exceptional slackness of the labour market. Prices refused to fall, and the customary wage of the agricultural labourer was insufficient to support both himself and those dependant on him. Nor was he able to establish a higher wage, for under pressure of poverty the small holder of land did more farm work himself with the help of his family and employed less hired labour than usual. Regard had to be paid to these facts, especially in the most afflicted tracts, when it became a question of closing or continuing the relief works. The condition of the young, the infirm and the aged also required increased attention. In the struggle for food these were the classes that suffered most, and to effectively relieve them became the chief care of the administration. The expedient of substituting cooked food for the money dole allowed by the codes to dependants of relief workers has already been mentioned. In the period now described the relief kitchen, as an adjunct to the relief work, came to be still more generally adopted, and may, without exaggeration, be said to have saved the lives of thousands of children. Under the original form of the piece-work or modified task-work system introduced in the North-Western Provinces and elsewhere the workers were expected to provide for their families from their earnings. But as the sad condition of the children and the neglect of the parents became more evident, it was found advisable to add the children's kitchen to the piece-work regulations. In Bengal and in the Central Provinces the relief kitchen in the last stage of the famine was also largely used apart from relief works as a form of gratuitous relief for necessitous persons in towns and villages. But this is anticipating the course of events.

Extension of gratuitous relief.

72. The expansion of gratuitous relief in the homes of the people in this period in Upper India was another natural consequence of the altered conditions of the famine. In the North-Western Provinces and Oudh the number of persons receiving such relief was 352,000 in the beginning of May and 470,000 at the end of July. In Bengal the numbers rose from 292,000 in May to 450,000 in the third week of July. In the Central Provinces the numbers rose during the period from 100,000 to 201,000. It has already been said that the extensive resort in the North-Western Provinces and in Bengal to this form of relief formed the subject of some

correspondence between the Government of India and the respective local Governments. The Government of the North Western Provinces thus described its policy in the matter :—

"It has been a constant instruction to the officers of this Government to bring no one on the village lists who either could support himself or who had relations accustomed to support him and still able to do so. The natural tendency has been for people to transfer their burdens to the State, and some firmness has been required to resist it. Mere physical appearance, which might be due to disease, was not held a sufficient test by itself, though it might deceive a superficial observer. Even in the tracts of greatest crop failure there were villages or holdings which yielded some outturn and benefited by the high prices of produce. In Bánda, a very acutely distressed district, the number on this form of relief on 3rd April was almost 4 per cent. of the population. On the same date Azamgarh, a poor district with a dense rural population (804·6 to the square mile), but very much less acutely distressed than Bánda, had only 0·16 of its population so relieved. Hardoi, which was distressed last year as well as this, had 2·4 per cent. The adjacent district of Sitapur, which was much better off, had only 0·4. In Allahabad, which contained some very impoverished tracts and which had also suffered last year, the district incidence was 2·2. Jaunpur, in spite of its dense rural population (816 to the square mile), required only 0·7 per cent., because distress was limited and less intense than in the worst districts. Gorakhpur did not suffer so severely as the Bundelkhand districts. In it the village relief was extended to only 0·5 of the population, whereas Jalaun showed 4·3 per cent. Later on in the season, as home resources became more exhausted and the circle of distress in each village widened, the home relief expanded, but its relation to the intensity of distress in each locality has always been maintained. The Lieutenant-Governor has always recognised the necessity for extreme care in the distribution of this form of relief, which carries with it no self-acting test, and is therefore specially liable to abuse."

73. The Government of Bengal succinctly put the case for Behar in the following words :—

"In England and Wales 2·85 per cent. of the entire population are in poor-houses or in receipt of out-door relief. In ordinary times it is probable that 3 per cent. of the population of Behar are entirely dependent on private charity. It should not then be a matter for surprise if in Behar, with the most congested and the poorest population in India or perhaps in the world, 4 to 5 per cent. of the population are unable to work and have nobody to maintain them in a famine year of unprecedently high prices and of failure of crops, admitted by all competent observers to be as great as that of 1873–74."

As regards other districts outside Behar, especially the Naddea district in the neighbourhood of Calcutta in which the numbers gratuitously relieved for a few weeks exceeded 10 per cent. of the population, the Government of Bengal admitted that sufficient discretion had not been exercised by the local authorities. The expedient of offering cooked food at kitchens instead of doles of money or grain was adopted with great effect. In a few weeks the number of persons receiving gratuitous relief in Naddea fell from 60,000 to 6,000.

74. In the Central Provinces the extension of gratuitous relief in the homes of the people and by means of poor-houses during May, June and July was necessitated by manifest signs of deterioration in the physical condition of the labouring classes, especially in that of the children, by the great difficulty of keeping open a sufficient number of relief works during the heavy rains experienced in this part of India and by the sickness and mortality among the workers which resulted from exposure to the inclemency of the weather. In instructions issued on the 2nd July, the Chief Commissioner thus described the circumstances which had to be met :—

"Suitable monsoon work cannot be provided in unlimited quantities, and while our public works programmes are thus necessarily restricted, a large body of labour, with its accompanying crowd of dependants, has been thrown out of employment by the closing of all tank work and other earth-work carried on under civil officers or with the aid of famine loans. When to this is added the effect of rising prices on such activity as local private charity has hitherto displayed, it is obvious that we must expect a considerable deepening of distress, and we must depend very largely for its removal on house-to-house relief in villages and towns. In most of the severely distressed districts, the numbers on this form of relief have for some weeks past been mounting rapidly, and they will no doubt continue to increase. In others, where this form of relief has hitherto not been thought necessary, or where it has not been extended over the whole district, the district officer should not hesitate to apply it wherever there is any sign of deterioration in the physical condition of the people."

Children's kitchens in the Central Provinces.

75. The establishment of relief kitchens at police stations and other convenient centres for the feeding mainly of children of parents unable to support them was also laid down in these instructions. During July the rapid increase in the death rate of particular localities showed how seriously privation and unwholesome food had impaired the vitality of the

poorer classes, and compelled the local Administration to multiply posts where persons in need of food might obtain relief. This was first taken in hand with vigour in the Jubbulpur Division, where the Commissioner described the children as being in many cases "reduced to mere skin and bone." Labouring men and women, he found, could earn no more than sufficed for their own food. "They have nothing for their children, who are practically left to graze in the "fields. It is commonly admitted by the people that the emaciated children one "sees in the kitchens have been subsisting entirely on wild indigo and similar "weeds for the past month." In the Seoni district in July last 59 kitchens were opened, in the Mandla district 20, in the Saugor district 25. A similar need of this kind of relief was recognised in the case of the huge district of Bilaspur, where distress was acute throughout 8,500 square miles and among a population of 1,100,000. The obstacles to communications were great in this tract of rice-swamps and forest, and in spite of enlarged establishments it was almost impossible to bring relief to every village and every home where it was required. Convenient centres where food could be obtained seemed in the circumstances the best expedient. To this was added a system of road patrols whose duty it was to convey to these centres or to the poor-houses any starving wanderers found on the roads. These instances will serve to explain the increasing resort to gratuitous relief in the Central Provinces seen in the relief statistics for the period under mention, and even more apparent in the figures for the next period, notwithstanding the improved agricultural outlook and the certainty of a good autumn harvest.

Position in Southern India.

76. The situation in Southern India during May, June and July differed from that of Central and Upper India. Here the rains were light and ill-distributed, and in the affected districts of the Deccan agriculture, except in favoured tracts, was more or less at a standstill. The difficulty of keeping relief-works open experienced in the Central Provinces did not exist here, and the demand for work on the part of the people was unabated In Madras at the end of April there were 201,000 persons on relief-works and 30,000 on gratuitous relief. At the end of July the relief-workers had risen to 557,000 and the numbers otherwise relieved to 250,000. Of the latter number 40,000 were weavers relieved at their craft. The great rise in the relief-work population has above been explained to be due in a great measure to injudicious relaxation of the labour-tests. The reasons for the great expansion of gratuitous relief are somewhat obscure. In the Ganjam district, where 96,000 persons at the end of July were thus relieved, the Uriya population is said to have an insuperable objection to appearing on relief-works. In the Deccan districts the system adopted in Madras of encouraging the relief-workers not to reside on the relief-works greatly reduced the "dependants" of workers to whom relief is given in connection with the works. And it may be conjectured that persons, who in other provinces would as "dependants" have received relief on the works, were in Madras relieved gratuitously in their homes. But a comparison of the Madras relief figures with those of the adjoining Bombay Deccan districts leads to the opinion that in Madras gratuitous relief was more freely given than in Bombay, and that the whole relief system was framed on very liberal lines. In Bombay, at the end of April, there were 373,000 persons on relief-works and 30,000 in receipt of gratuitous relief. At the end of July the relief-work population in that Presidency numbered 352,000 and the persons gratuitously relieved 56,000. The decline in the relief-workers appears to have been due to the strict enforcement of labour-tests and the concentration of the workers on a comparatively small number of large works. The moderate increase in the numbers on gratuitous relief also indicates the cautious spirit with which in this Presidency famine has been administered.

Analysis of relief at end of July.

77. In paragraph 49 of the narrative the distribution of the persons relieved in each Province at the end of April under each main head of relief was analytically shown. A similar analysis of the relief population at the end of July is required

to complete the notice of this period, and is given below :—

Provinces.	Employed on relief-works.			Employed on test-works.	Total employed on works.	Gratuitously relieved.			Grand Total.
	Workers.	Dependants.	Total.			In poor-houses or kitchens.	In their homes.	Total.	
Madras	536,647	19,894	556,541	530	557,071	36,486	213,420	249,906	806,977
Bombay	285,585	66,792	352,377	...	352,377	2,415	54,188	56,603	408,980
Bengal	164,574	6,974	171,548	1,855	173,403	36,848	356,638	388,486	561,889
North-Western Provinces and Oudh.	83,263	17,406	100,669	1,199	101,868	43,219	360,389	403,608	505,476
Punjab	21,120	2,792	23,912	...	23,912	1,123	10,775	11,998	35,910
Central Provinces ...	348,944	53,150	402,094	...	402,094	32,942	167,827	200,769	602,863
Burma	26,586	...	26,586	...	26,586	...	7,211	7,211	33,797
Berar	17,012	...	17,012	...	17,012	3,455	8,462	11,917	28,929
Total	1,483,731	167,008	1,650,739	3,584	1,654,323	156,488	1,174,010	1,330,498	2,984,821
Native States.									
Hyderabad	15,587	...	15,587	...	15,587	...	1,902	1,902	17,489
Central India	45,125	...	45,125	...	45,125	...	18,172	18,172	63,297
Rajputana	3,369	...	3,369	...	3,369	...	7,321	7,321	10,690
Total	64,081	...	64,081	...	64,081	...	27,395	27,395	91,476
Grand Total ...	1,547,812	167,008	1,714,820	3,584	1,718,404	156,488	1,201,405	1,357,893	3,076,297

VIII.—The fourth period.—The close of the famine.

78. This last period is still incomplete, as in no Province at the present moment have relief operations actually been brought to a close ; though in most parts of India their closure is at most a matter of a very few weeks. It is permissible therefore in this part of the narrative to be brief. The contraction of relief operations will be seen from the table below :—

Province.	Numbers on relief at end of each fortnight.				
	Second half of July.	First half of August.	Second half of August.	First half of September.	Second half of September.
Madras	806,977	694,745	593,160	354,444	171,843
Bombay	408,980	403,442	435,776	464,586	352,610
Bengal	561,889	448,807	335,776	92,287	18,018
North-Western Provinces and Oudh	505,476	466,821	397,707	241,630	120,606
Punjab	35,910	26,499	17,547	4,929	833
Central Provinces	602,863	577,758	563,833	618,308	654,852
Burma	33,797	26,037	21,175	18,027	17,072
Berar	28,927	14,947	10,955	6,779	8,609
Total	2,984,821	2,659,056	2,375,979	1,800,990	1,344,443
Native States.					
Hyderabad	17,489	18,435	21,275	22,863	24,446
Central India	63,297	48,349	49,103	26,656	25,076
Rajputana	10,690	8,435	6,042	5,741	3,657
Total	91,476	75,272	76,420	55,260	53,179
Grand Total	3,076,297	2,734,328	2,452,379	1,856,250	1,397,622

79. In Upper India, the maturing of the early rain crops in September, and the consequent cheapening of rice, Indian corn and other autumn food-grains on which the poorer classes largely depend, the better demand for field labour, and the improvement in the general outlook, have enabled the Governments of Bengal and the North-Western Provinces and Oudh to rapidly close the relief-works, and to restrict relief to the very young, the aged and the infirm, who have to rely on the support of others. In the first week of September, the population on relief-works in Bengal had fallen to 32,000 and on gratuitous relief to 192,000. On the same date in the North-Western Provinces and Oudh the relief-works population had fallen to 16,000, and the numbers in receipt of gratuitous relief to 256,000. Since then further progress has been made in reducing the gratuitous lists. In both provinces, the procedure in this respect has been identical. Villages in which early kharif crops predominate have first been operated on; in such villages gratuities equivalent to relief for a week or fourteen days have been given to the poor on the gratuitous list, and they have been informed that they must now manage for themselves or rely on others for support, as in pre-famine times. This is inevitable, if a permanent poor law in India is to be avoided. Villages in which the crops are later in maturing are then to be similarly dealt with, and it is anticipated that by the end of October in both provinces relief will cease. In the Punjab the numbers on relief have for some weeks past been very small, and no great hardship would result from a complete cessation of relief. In Burma relief may be required until the end of the year; but as it is chiefly given in the form of work on remunerative canal irrigation projects, this is of no great consequence. In Madras and Bombay the copious rainfall of September has changed the situation from one of grave anxiety to one of hope. Relief in Madras is expected to cease in the present month. In Bombay, distress, to judge by the high death-rates of the Deccan Districts, and the persistence of high prices, appears to be somewhat more acute than in Madras, especially among the hill tribes, and relief may here have to continue longer.

Relief ceases in most provinces.

80. In the Central Provinces the physical condition of the people is still deplorably bad, the general death-rate of the province in July and August extremely high, and relief on a large scale will in all probability be necessary until the end of the year. The numbers on relief are now in excess of what they were at the end of July, and increasing resort is found necessary to the two expedients of relief in the homes of the people and relief-kitchens, described in the last section of this narrative. The numbers on relief works at the close of September have fallen to 263,985, while the numbers gratuitously relieved in poor-houses, kitchens and in their homes has risen to 391,867. In Bilaspur 9 per cent. of the population is thus gratuitously relieved, in Jubbulpur 7 per cent., in Damoh 9 per cent., in Mandla 7 per cent., and in several other districts between 4 and 6 per cent. The extension of village relief and the multiplication of kitchens have in fact been the principal feature of the relief operations in the last two months, and the latest report of the Chief Commissioner is to the effect that "no appreciable "reduction in the numbers on gratuitous relief can be expected for some time "to come, even in the districts which show the highest totals, while there are "others, such as Saugor, Betul, Mandla and Chhindwara, in which further additions "must be looked for." Of children's kitchens he writes that "They are proving "most useful and effective. It has been established by experience that in most "cases parents cannot be trusted to feed their children out of the doles granted "them for the purpose, and that in severely distressed tracts the village relief "system is therefore by itself inadequate, and requires to be supplemented by "special measures to secure that the children are properly fed." The deterioration in the general health of the population of these provinces is particularly marked, since the commencement of the rainy season, and occasions grave anxiety. The death-rate for the province in July was 6·47 per mille, and in August 8·35 per mille, equivalent to annual ratios of 77·6 and 100·2 per mille respectively. The following passages from the reports of the Chief Commissioner for the two months in question deal with this subject, and seem to summarise all that can be said upon it. Of the mortality of July he wrote:—

Position in the Central Provinces.

"The break in the rains with which the month commenced, and which lasted throughout a third of it, was not only in itself adverse to health, restoring conditions of drought and heat after a heavy and general downpour, but also deprived the labouring classes of that employment to seek which many thousands had left the relief works. The savings they had made were soon exhausted, while prices, which might have been expected to fall with a continuance of favourable rain, remained extremely high, or even (in the general apprehension of renewed failure of crops) rose still higher than at the end of the hot weather. The climatic conditions of the rainy season are at all times adverse to health, and they were particularly so to persons enfeebled by long continued privation, and exposed without sufficient clothing or shelter to great changes of temperature and heavy falls of rain. The mortality of the month is chiefly ascribed to bowel diseases and fevers, the normal complaints of the season. The former were probably aggravated by the use of unwholesome food, as pointed out in the monthly report, while the latter were particularly prevalent in consequence of the return of heat during the break in the rains, and the sudden lowering of temperature when the monsoon rainfall recommenced."

Reporting still greater mortality in August, he wrote :—

"This general increase, characterising alike those districts where distress is most acute and those where it is (comparatively) less severe, points to a common cause which is not wholly the pressure of scarcity, but is climatic in its origin. The copious rainfall of the month, with chills due to the fall of temperature caused thereby, has undoubtedly produced a large excess of deaths from fevers, dysentery and diarrhœa. The use of the vegetables common in the rainy season—various forms of gourds and cucumbers—has probably added to the virulence of bowel complaints. But, quite apart from the causes affecting the general population, there can be no doubt that the deplorable mortality of the month (in all years one of the most unhealthy of the twelve) is mainly to be ascribed to the effect of unfavourable conditions on constitutions weakened by continued privation. Although all through the month every effort was made to extend village and kitchen relief to those in need, it was not possible to counteract the effects of a continued scanty allowance of food in the case of the many thousands of persons who had not taken advantage of the relief offered them by Government on works, but had preferred to remain at home looking after their crops or accepting private employment, at a low and insufficient wage. These are persons whom no form of Government relief, except such as would completely take the place of private employment, could reach."

81. Elsewhere in this narrative mention has been made of the fact that the famine in the Central Provinces represents the cumulative weight of three bad years on the agricultural population. That this has had much to do with the enfeebled condition of the people there can be little doubt. As regards the adequacy of the relief measures which have been taken, it is perhaps sufficient here to say that they have been on a very extensive scale, that, although occasional mistakes may have been made, as is inevitable where the field of operations is so large, they have, as a whole, at each point of time been considered by the local administration to be sufficient for the requirements of the situation, and that by August 1897 the direct expenditure on relief incurred in the Central Provinces by the State from November 1896 amounted to not less than Rs. 1,20,00,000 (Rx. 1,200,000) besides large suspensions of land-revenue and loans to landowners and cultivators. It may also be remarked that in these provinces famine has been very difficult not only to combat, but in its earlier stages to correctly diagnose. Distress has declared itself or deepened in particular tracts with great rapidity and with no premonitory symptoms. From the Narbudda Valley districts in the west the centre of intense distress suddenly shifted in May to Bilaspur in the east, and scarcely were relief arrangements enlarged to meet the danger in Bilaspur, when in July the Mandla and Betul districts in the central highlands called for increased attention. Next the Saugor and Damoh districts in the Vindhyan Hills showed in August by a rising death-rate that there pressure was increasing. This peculiarity has greatly increased the difficulty of the situation and hampered the local Administration. It may however be permissible to hope that the worst is over, as good rain crops are on the ground, and the cold weather sowings are being successfully commenced.

Central India.

82. In Central India, distress is reported to have greatly abated in the Baghelkhand and Bundelkhand Agencies, where crops promise well and prices are falling. It has almost ceased in the Gwalior State, and in those of the Rajputana States in which relief measures were necessary. Throughout Rajputana, as throughout Central India, the agricultural outlook could not be better In Hyderabad, the situation till quite recently was very much the same as in the Madras Deccan country, and matters did not improve until the heavy rainfall of September.

83. To complete the review of this closing stage of the famine, the disposition of the persons in receipt of relief at the end of September is given below :—

Analysis of relief at end of September.

Provinces.	Employed on Relief Works.			Employed on test works.	Total employed on works.	Gratuitously Relieved.			Grand Total.
	Workers.	Dependants.	Total.			In poor-houses or kitchens.	In their homes.	Total.	
Madras	92,942	8,477	101,419	67	101,486	11.162	59,195	70,357	171,843
Bombay	206,157	50,188	256,345	285	256,630	3,827	92,153	95,980	352,610
Bengal	9,410	—	9,410	—	9,410	3,354	5,254	8,668	18,018
North-Western Provinces and Oudh.	—	—	—	—	—	5,017	115,589	120,606	120,606
Punjab	—	—	—	—	—	623	210	833	833
Central Provinces ...	229 972	32.920	262,892	93	262,985	44,155	347,712	391,867	654,852
Burma	13,320	—	13,320	—	13,320	—	3,752	3,752	17,072
Berar	2,135	—	2,135	—	2,135	2,484	3,990	6,474	8,609
Total	553,936	91,585	645,521	445	645.966	70,622	627,855	698,477	1,344,443
Native States.									
Hyderabad	22,251	—	22,251	—	22.251	—	2.195	2,195	24,446
Central India ...	8,065	—	8,065	—	8,065	—	17,011	17,011	25,076
Rajputana	340	—	340	—	340	—	3,317	3,317	3,657
Total	30,656	—	30,656	—	30,656	—	22,523	22,523	53,179
Grand Total ...	584,592	91,585	676,177	445	676,622	70,622	650,378	721,000	1,397,622

IX.—The mortality of the famine.

84. It is impossible at the present time to deal with this subject completely or satisfactorily, yet it is of too great importance and interest to be entirely omitted from any narrative of the late famine. The latest published death-rate returns for the several provinces, in which the mortality is classified acccording to causes of death, are for the month of July 1897. The approximate death-rate for each month in each affected district has been obtained under special arrangements up to August. But in this return the causes of death are not shown. Imperfect as the materials are, they are unfortunately sufficient for the conclusion that a considerable excess in the mortality rate has attended the late famine. The relation of the mortality of India to famine was carefully considered in 1881 by the Famine Commission, and their remarks are very opposite to the present occasion :—

High mortality and periods of scarcity are concomitant.

"The hope that any human endeavours," write the Famine Commission, "will altogether prevent an increase of mortality during a severe famine is untenable. It is impossible for the State entirely to counteract the effect of high prices, the cessation of wages, the disturbance of the ordinary routine of life, the general results of shortened food-supply to millions of people. No imaginable system of relief will completely meet all the various degrees of privation and suffering which a famine produces, and which are all more or less prejudicial to the public health and life, though many are too indefinite and obscure to be dealt with by any machinery of official charity, however elaborate and well contrived. There must always be suffering and want which will escape notice ; and however extensive be the measures of public aid, and however reasonable be the terms on which it is offered, there will always be classes who from fixed habits or social institutions of various sorts, or from their personal character or ignorance, will neither help themselves nor be helped, and who, though they suffer from extreme want, will linger on without applying for or accepting relief till it is too late to save their lives."

Report of the Famine Commission, Part I., paragraph 83.

85. The Famine Commissioners proceed to show that not only is the general death-rate of India when compared with that of England high, but it is liable to far greater variations. They remark that the yearly death-rate of many

Indian towns rises occasionally for many months together to rates varying from 40 to 100 per mille, and even higher; and they give as a typical instance the epidemic of malarial fever which in the North-Western Provinces and Oudh in 1879, when no scarcity whatever existed and prices were moderate, raised the death-rate in some districts from its ordinary total of two or three per mille per month to nearly 40, the death-rate for the whole province of October 1879 from the normal of 3·4 to 10 per mille, and of the whole year from the normal of 23 to 45 per mille. In this case famine was absent. But it is a well-ascertained law, the Famine Commissioners remark, that pestilence accompanies famine, and that the two are the twin-offspring of drought, "which, while it withers the crops, "exposes the diminished water-supply to pollution," and brings about "abnormal "conditions of temperature and humidity." Both from these causes and because great and prolonged scarcity must necessarily impair the general health of the population and render it an easy prey to disease, the occurrence of a high death-rate in a famime year is to be expected: and it is impossible to resolve the general death-rate into the portions due respectively to abnormal sickness and disease and to privations from want of sufficient food. An attempt has been made in the recent famine to have all deaths directly due to starvation, and also—in some provinces—indirectly due to the effects of privation, separately returned. The results in a way are satisfactory, as, with the one exception of the Central Provinces, no province in India has returned in any month more than one or two, at most, verified deaths from starvation. Usually the return has been blank. Reserving the returns of the Central Provinces for separate discussion, it may be said in explanation of the returns of the other provinces that village inspection and relief have in the late famine been so widely extended as to ensure food being brought within the reach of all persons of settled habitat. Deaths in which privation or starvation has been suspected have virtually been confined to stray cases of unknown wanderers found dead in the open country and of persons dying after admission to a poor-house. In such cases verification of the cause of death has not been found possible, and they have properly been excluded from the return.

Attempted recording of privation deaths.

86. In the Central Provinces this rule of exclusion was not adopted, and the reporting agency, which consists of village watchmen and subordinate police officers, was permitted or directed to return as deaths due to starvation or privation all cases in which starvation or privation might be conjectured from circumstances more or less general. In the earlier months of the famine the large number of deaths returned in these provinces as due to these causes attracted attention and the matter was looked into. It was then found that the returns included many doubtful cases and many cases which could not on any theory be properly ascribed to these causes. In one district all deaths occurring in a poor-house were so returned. In another district the same practice was followed with regard to the deaths of persons on the village gratuitous relief lists. Deaths of wanderers on the roads or in the fields, which were as likely to have been due to cholera as to privation, were frequently returned under the latter head. Commenting on these and similar errors the Commissioner of Jubbulpur wrote in May to the following effect: "The determination of whether a death is or is not due to privation is a "delicate and difficult operation, and I do not think that our reporting agency "(village watchmen and subordinate police officers) can be relied upon to "discriminate these deaths satisfactorily. It may be said indeed that proper "verification should make the cause of death certain, but where, as is the case with "most deaths from starvation, the victims are wanderers without friends or "companions who can give any information regarding them, any real verification is "quite out of the question, and I do not think that any great weight should be "attached to statistics given under this head." The general correctness of this view is indisputable. It is unhappily certain that the mortality directly due to privation or starvation has been very much greater in the Central Provinces than elsewhere. Famine of the acutest type has existed in these provinces for months. They have been overrun with famished refugees from Native States, and the practice of wandering has prevailed there to an infinitely greater extent than in any other part of British India. All these circumstances have been productive of the

Incorrectness of such returns.

mortality specially associated with the privations of famine. But there is no correct return of such mortality in existence, and it is important to recognise the fact.

The death rate in each Province examined.

87. The general death-rate of the population in each affected district in British India for each month from October 1896 to August 1897 is given in Appendix III. The results for each province may be briefly noticed. In Madras the excess mortality over the normal has been slight, and such excess as is observable in the returns is confined to the Ganjam and Vizagapatam districts and to the Bhadrachalam subdivision of the Godaveri district, and is chiefly due to cholera. In the four affected Deccan districts the death rates in successive months have been more generally below than above the normal. In Bombay up to April 1897 there was nothing in the monthly death-rates of these districts to distinguish the year as one of scarcity. But from May onwards the death-rates, as the following figures show, have been abnormally high, even if deaths from cholera be excluded :—

Madras.

Bombay.

—	Monthly death-rate 1897 from all causes				Monthly death-rate in 1897 excluding cholera.			
	May.	June	July.	August.	May.	June.	July.	August.
Ahmednagar	3·32	3·50	6·86	7·18	3·32	3·38	5·20	5·68
Khandesh	2·95	3·17	3·62	7·32	2·95	3·10	3·12	6·08
Nasik	3·23	5·25	6·54	8·06	3·23	3·69	5·41	6·99
Poona	2·59	5 72	10·10	7·18	2 55	3·63	8·22	5·82
Satara	7·12	5·81	5·82	5·52	3·62	3·65	4·52	5·19
Sholapur	4·12	3·96	7·72	5·78	3·35	3·41	5·25	5·36
Bijapur	6·87	4·56	5·25	5·18	3·75	3·86	4·75	5·18

Plague has been rife in several of these districts, and owing to the protracted break in the rains in July and August general climatic conditions have been very unfavourable to health. Prices have been persistently higher in the Bombay than in the Madras Deccan, and at the end of August they continued to rise, while in Upper India a fall had set in. Until the period of tension was terminated by the opportune and heavy rainfall of September, there was undoubtedly much privation among the lower classes of these districts. Up to June the good physical condition and the well-nurtured appearance of the applicants for relief, and of the relief labourers, in the Deccan districts of Bombay was frequently remarked on by the Sanitary Commissioner in his inspection tours. Since then his reports have noticed signs of deterioration in this respect, and his observations appear to be borne out by the increase in the mortality of the population.

Bengal.

88. In Bengal, the public health in the affected districts—even in the worst parts of North Behar—has been singularly good, evidencing the comparative shortness of the famine, and the good condition of the people at the time of its commencement in November last, and also evidencing the effective character of the relief measures taken by the Government of Bengal. The province had not been afflicted by a continuous succession of bad harvests, and through the early setting in of the rains in Bengal, and the obtaining of an early autumn harvest, it has been the first to pass out of the late disastrous season into one of assured prosperity. The August death-rates in some of the districts were high, notably in some districts of Chota Nagpur.* But the excess over the normal is in these cases due to a severe epidemic of cholera.

	August death-rate.
*Palamau	6·43
Manbhum	4·49
Hazaribagh	10·51
Lohardagga	12·07

89. The death-rates of ten districts known to have been the most seriously distressed in the North-Western Provinces and Oudh are, month by month, as follows :—

North-Western Provinces and Oudh.

Division.	District.	October.	November.	December.	January.	February.	March.	April.	May.	June.	July.	August.
Allahabad ...	Banda	4·20	4·39	4·71	5·10	4·81	5·09	5·23	4·73	3·60	2·62	2·61
	Hamirpur	8·06	6·13	5·35	5·03	3·64	3·41	2·15	2·97	4·97	3·80	6·62
	Allahabad	2·37	2·08	3·34	3·55	3·48	5·40	4·41	2·98	3·09	2·45	2·70
	Jhansi	7·37	5·86	5·29	4·92	4 16	3·73	2·59	2·73	3·25	3·18	4·40
	Jalaun	3·24	3·01	3·29	3·29	2·75	3·09	2·62	2·34	3·67	4·39	6·19
Lucknow ...	Lucknow	2·01	2·25	3·20	3·87	3·33	3·80	3·91	3·41	3·06	4·89	6·00
	Unao	1·96	1·73	2·59	3·63	3·31	3·86	3·52	3·08	2·34	2·81	3·26
	Rai Bareli	2·01	2·37	3·71	4·81	4·38	5·42	5·21	4·01	2·95	2·94	3·64
	Sitapur	2·90	2·63	2·61	2·52	2·30	2·49	3·68	3·39	2 96	2·70	5·11
	Hardoi	4·43	2·76	3·49	4·39	4·0	4·71	5·27	3·51	2·95	4·37	5·72

Of these death-rates it may be said that though, taken collectively, they represent a mortality considerably in excess of the average over a series of years, there is no district in the table of which the death-rate of one month, at least, of the series is not below the normal for the month. This appears to connect the fluctuations with climatic conditions. It may also be remarked that there is little or no sign in these death-rates of progressive pressure of distress. The death-rates are collectively lowest in May and June 1897, when famine was at its height. They rose again in August, when food and employment became more abundant. The highest death-rates in the series occurred in October 1896. Enquiry made at the time showed that in the districts of Hamirpur and Jhansi where these exceptional death-rates were recorded malarial fever was very prevalent. Again the rise to 6·62 per mille in August 1897 in Hamirpur, and to 6·19 in Jalaun in the same month, was largely due to cholera. The high rates returned in March and April in the Allahabad district were similarly occasioned. It is also to be noticed that the highest death-rates in the table are more than paralleled by the rates returned in October and November 1896, by four districts* in which distress was acknowledged to be slight, and where the high mortality was undoubtedly due to unfavourable climatic conditions and not to privation.

	Per mille. October.	Per month. November.
*Bareilly	8·33	6·07
Moradabad ...	6·90	4·14
Shahjehanpur ...	7·59	4·14
Pilibhit	9·10	7·16

90. In the affected tracts of the Punjab the monthly death-rates have been exceptionally low from the beginning to the end of the famine. Even in the Hissar district in which severe distress prevailed, the mortality from October 1896 to August 1897 is less than that for an average of years. The general health of the province has been extremely good and there has been a singular absence of malarial fever which in most years is very deadly in parts of the Punjab in the autumn months. As regards therefore the Punjab no exceptional mortality is associated with the late famine.

Punjab.

91. The monthly death-rate per mille of the population of the Central Provinces from October 1896 to August 1897 is as follows :—

Central Provinces.

1896.			1897.							
October.	November.	December.	January.	February.	March.	April.	May.	June.	July.	August.
4·86	3·77	3·72	3·84	3·59	3·77	4·04	5·93	7·53	6·47	8·35

The annual death-rate for the province in the three years before 1896 was, respectively, 27·70 per mille for 1893, 37·22 per mille for 1894, and 36·75 per mille for 1895. The monthly rates given above represent a mortality larger in excess of these annual rates. But it is to be mentioned that the death-rate commenced to rise early in 1896 and that the death-rate for that year was 49·05. Causes therefore were at work injuriously affecting the public health of the population of the province before the failure of the crops in September of that year plunged it into intense distress.

92. The monthly death-rates in the several districts of the Central Provinces during the period covered by famine operations present extraordinary fluctuations. In October 1896, the death-rate was 50 per cent. or more in excess of the normal rate for the month, in nine districts out of the eighteen into which the provinces are divided. The districts showing an excess rate lay chiefly in the Narbudda Valley, the highest rates being in Damoh (10·2), Saugor (8·1), Jubbulpur (7·4), and Mandla (6·0). In November there was an improvement, as in five districts only was the recorded rate for the month 50 per cent. or more above the normal rate. From December to April the number of such districts varied between eight and nine, the highest rates recorded in February being in Jubbulpur (6·7), and Mandla (7·1) ; and in March in Jubbulpur (7·7), Mandla (6·7), Balaghat (6·7), and Bilaspur (5·2). The addition of Bilaspur in March to the districts with the greatest mortality, is significant, as it indicates the spread of severe distress from the Nerbudda Valley, and the Satpura plateau to the rice-growing plain of Chhattisgarh. In April, cholera was very destructive in several districts, and in the two following months greatly increased in virulence, 15,600 deaths being recorded as due to that cause in May, and 21,000 in June. The mortality from all causes in some districts was accordingly very high, six districts in May returning a death-rate between 7 and 8 per mille per month, and four districts in June returning a death-rate above 10 per mille. Excluding deaths from cholera the districts with the highest death-rate in each month from April onwards are as follows :—

	April.	May.	June.	July.	August.
Number of districts with mortality from all causes 50 per cent. above normal ...	8	13	16	15	16
Districts with highest death-rate, excluding cholera deaths	Saugor (4·7)	Jubbulpur (5·2)	Jubbulpur (5·0)	Saugor (8·0)	Saugor (11·5)
	Narsinghpur (4·6)	Saugor (5·8)	Saugor (8·5)	Seoni (8·0)	Seoni (12·1)
	Bilaspur (5·7)	Damoh (5·2)	Mandla (6·9)	Mandla (14·2)	Mandla (16·1)
		Mandla (5·1)	Narsinghpur (5·9)	Narsinghpur (5·8)	Narsinghpur (7·1
		Narsinghpur (5·3)	Nimar (5·4)	Betul (6·4)	Betul (11·5)
		Nimar (5·3)	Raipur (5·7)	Raipur (6·2)	Raipur (9·5)
		Bilaspur (5·0)	Bilaspur (6·8)	Bilaspur (9·4)	Bilaspur (12·4)
		Hoshangabad (5·1)			

93. The continuous rise in the death-rate of so many districts after the disturbing element of cholera mortality has been eliminated, is one of the most perplexing questions which have arisen in connection with the famine in the Central Provinces. It has occurred at the very time when the relief organisation was most complete and extensive and the relief expenditure of the State at its highest point. It was shown in a preceding section of this narrative that strenuous efforts were made in this stage of the famine to extend village relief and multiply children's kitchens. But among the hills and forests which are the characteristics of the greater portion of the provinces the difficulties of the relieving officers, especially in the unhealthy season of the rains, were far greater than in the plains of Upper India or the Deccan, and they have

had to deal with aboriginal races who are proverbially shy and distrustful. In the more open and settled country the petty cultivators seem to have clung to their homes with extraordinary pertinacity, and to have accepted great privations rather than seek for relief. It is comparatively easy to secure to relief workers a sufficient subsistence, and to relieve in their homes the aged, the infirm and the young, who are clearly incapable of work and who are fit recipients of gratuitous relief. But it is very difficult to deal with persons who are capable of work who actually have employment in their fields and villages, but who cannot earn enough to properly support themselves and their families with food at famine prices. The Chief Commissioner has summed up this difficulty in a passage which, though it has been already quoted, may be repeated:—"It has not," he says, "been possible to counteract the effects of a scanty allowance of "food in the case of the many thousands of persons who had not taken advantage "of the relief offered them, but had preferred to remain at home, looking after "their crops, or accepting private employment at a low and insufficient wage. "There are persons whom no form of Government relief, except such as would "completely take the place of private employment, could reach." Such persons, though their vitality may be low and their physical powers enfeebled, can drag through the healthy months when existence is easy. But they fall a ready prey to malaria and damp in the unhealthy months of the rains, and to dysentery and other similar diseases which then prevail. The classified returns of deaths for July show that out of 61,445 deaths in these provinces from all causes, 35,475 were recorded as due to fevers, 8,638 to dysentery and diarrhœa, and 5,243 to cholera. The deaths from fevers and dysentery and diarrhœa were much in excess of the normal number for the month. The August returns, when they appear, will probably show a similar excess in the mortality under these two heads.*

94. In the Berars the monthly death rates of the six districts into which that province is divided have shown little excess over the normal mortality of the month, and where excess is noticed it is due partly to deaths among wandering immigrants from the Central Provinces, but chiefly to deaths from cholera. This is the explanation of the high rates recorded in August in Amraoti (8·0), Akola (11·2), and Basim (7·8), districts, in which the general condition of the resident population was good or fair, and in which such distress as at one time existed had pretty well disappeared. In the distressed districts of Upper Burma cholera has also caused the death rates to rise in particular months, but, on the whole, they have not been high. It is, however, to be observed that the machinery for death registration is as yet imperfect in this part of British India, and the returns are not to be relied on. From Native States no reliable information on the subject is forthcoming, but from the miserable condition of the crowds of wanderers from Bundelkhand and Baghelkhand who flocked to the poorhouses in the Narbudda valley districts of the Central Provinces, it may be conjectured that the mortality in the affected parts of Central India has been high. It could not well be otherwise. The drought in those tracts was fully as intense as in British Bundelkhand, and the relief arrangements were necessarily less complete than in British territory.

Berar.

Upper Burma.

Native States.

X. *Statistics of cost and relief.*

95. The direct expenditure from the revenues of British India incurred in the relief of distress from the 1st November 1896 to the end of September 1897 may be approximately taken at Rs. 6,80,00,000 (Rx. 6,800,000). This, however, is only

The cost of the famine.

* Since this was written further information has been received from the Central Provinces which goes to show that a special type of malarial fever of a very fatal kind has prevailed in an epidemic form during the late rains in these provinces. There is evidence to the effect that mortality has been abnormally high, not only among the poorest classes, but also among the well-to-do, and that villages have had conspicuously high death-rates in which no emaciated person could be found. Extracts from this evidence are given in a Note at the end of this narrative.

the expenditure which under the standing financial rules is exhibited in the accounts under the head "Famine Relief." Much expenditure which is indirectly due to famine, such as compensation to menial Government servants or to soldiers for dearness of food, additions to existing civil establishments on account of the pressure of work, additions to medical establishments, and the like, go under other expenditure heads, and are not specifically charged to Famine Relief. A very important form of relief, namely, loans and advances to landlords and cultivators, with the object of providing employment on works of land improvements in distressed tracts, or for the purchase of seed and cattle, does not appear under "Famine Relief, but under the Debt head, in the financial accounts. According to the returns made by Local Governments up to the end of August, the disbursements on account of famine loans amounted to Rs. 1,28,77,000 (Rx. 1,287,700). Another consequence of famine is the decreased yield of many heads of revenue; but the only one which here claims notice is that of land-revenue, since suspensions of the land-revenue demand are an integral part of famine relief administration. According to the returns of the Local Governments, land revenue to the amount of Rs. 1,80,53,000 (Rx. 1,805,300), falling due between the 1st November 1896 and the end of August 1897, has been suspended. A good deal of this will in all probability have eventually to be remitted. It cannot well be otherwise. In districts where famine has been most intense, the small landowners will recommence the cultivation of their holdings not only without resources beyond their agricultural implements and cattle, but heavily in debt to the State for land revenue and for loans and advances. Even with good seasons the struggle to regain prosperity will be severe, and in such cases a lenient policy in the matter of arrears of land revenue is obviously the only one to be pursued.

The cost distributed by provinces.

96. Distributed by Provinces the direct expenditure on famine relief, the amounts loaned to landholders and cultivators, and the land revenue suspensions, so far as at present reported, appear as follows :—

Provinces.	Direct expenditure on famine relief to end of September.	Loans and advances to 31st August.	Land revenue suspended to 31st August.
	Rs.	Rs.	Rs.
Madras	91,00,000	16,43,000	28,70,000
Bombay	1,11,00,000	46,68,000	1,56,000
Bengal	1,13,00,000	11,22,595	*Nil.*
North-Western Provinces and Oudh	1,95,00,000	18,60,336	1,02,80,000
Punjab	18,00,000	7,53,200	16,46,000
Central Provinces	1,41,00,000	26,98,000	31,01,000
Burma	11,00,000	1,32,000	*Nil.*
Total	6,80,00,000	1,28,77,131	1,80,53,500

As illustrating differences of system in different Provinces, it may be noticed that in Madras the revenue suspensions have been extensive and in Bombay very small; on the other hand, the sums advanced to the landholders in the form of loans has been much larger in Bombay than in Madras. It is reported by the Government of Bombay that every precaution has been taken to ensure loans and advances being applied by the recipients to the objects for which they have been obtained, and that small land improvements of the nature of wells and tanks and reclamation of waste have been vigorously carried out through such funds. But for this it might be surmised that the State by lending money out of one pocket had managed to recover on account of the other. At the beginning of the famine the Government of Bombay anticipated that large suspensions of land revenue might be necessary, but as time went on, the cultivators were found to be considerably better off than was anticipated, and the land revenue seems to have been collected without difficulty or resort to coercive processes.

Comparison of cost with cost of former famines.

97. Compared with the expenditure on other great famines the expenditure on the late famine cannot be regarded as other than moderate. In the Behar Famine of 1873–74, in which a population of about fourteen millions was affected, but which is described by the Famine Commission as "a famine of unusual brevity, and of no exceptional severity," the sum of Rs. 6,61,00,000 (Rx. 6,610,000) was spent. In the terrible Madras Famine of 1876–78, in which a population of about ten millions was severely, and a further population of nine millions, slightly affected, the expenditure was Rs. 6,30,00,000 (Rx. 6,300,000). In the Bombay Famine of the same year, in which a population of six millions was severely, and a further population of four millions. slightly affected, the expenditure was Rs. 1,14,00,000 (Rx. 1,140,000). Of these three famines, the Bombay Famine of 1876–78 is the only one which in point of economical and efficient administration of relief, is comparable with the famine of the present year. In the late famine, a population in British India of forty-five millions was severely, and a further population of twelve millions was slightly affected. Relief has been given without stint or limitation, though subject to recognized tests and conditions, for a sum which, even should it reach Rx. 7,300,000 by the time relief operations are over in all Provinces, will yet be only Rx. 700,000 in excess of what was spent on the Behar Famine of 1873–74. If it be the case, as has been stated by the Government of Bengal, that the famine of this year in Behar was as severe as that of 1873–74, an excellent standard of comparison exists. The Government of Bengal has in 1896–97 relieved at one-sixth of the cost and in an admittedly adequate manner the same area and population which was relieved in 1873–74 at the cost of Rs. 6,61,00,000. Much of the very large expenditure in 1873–74 was due to special preparations which the Government, fearing an absolute dearth of food in North Behar, undertook by importing rice from Burma and transporting it to the famine districts. Such operations, even if they were necessary in 1873–74, have now been rendered obsolete by the great extension of railways and the improvement of road communications throughout Bengal, and particularly in Behar. But apart from this great item of expense in the Behar famine of 1873–74, there is clear evidence that in other ways the similar famine of 1896–97 has been much more satisfactorily administered. In 1873–74 at least 25 per cent. of the total population of the severely and slightly affected tracts were in receipt of relief for over 7 months,* and in the worst tracts this percentage was largely exceeded. This year the numbers on relief in the five districts of North Behar in no month exceeded 9·5 per cent. of the total population of the distressed areas, and for the 8 months from February to August they averaged less than 7 per cent. That this measure of relief has been ample has been nowhere disputed, and it seems to be conclusively established by the lowness of the death-rate. From this the extent to which relief given in the Behar famine of 1873–74 erred on the side of profusion may be inferred.

* Famine Commission's Report, Part III., page 145.

The ratio of the persons relieved to the total population.

98. The Behar case therefore shows that in a famine which does not extend beyond 9 months or a year, which, though it may be severe, is not intense, and which finds the people in good condition, not more than from 7 to 9 per cent. of the population should at the outside require relief. The rule is a very general one, as the ratio will be exceeded if famine be intense, and it will prove too high if distress is not severe. Taking the population of the distressed areas in British India in the late famine at 45½ millions, 6·5 per cent. were in receipt of relief from January to August, and 8 per cent. in the two months of May and June before the rains. In the North-Western Provinces and Oudh, nearly 10 per cent. of the population of the distressed areas were on relief in February, but the average for the 8 months from January to August was only 6 per cent. In the Central Provinces, the ratio for the 8 months was 7 per cent., and in May 9 per cent. In Bombay, the ratio was 9 per cent. in March and April, when relief was at its maximum. The district ratios are still more instructive, as showing the length to which it may be necessary in cases of intense distress to extend relief.

In Bengal, the highest ratio was attained in the Champaran district, where 15 per cent. of the population of the distressed area were in receipt of relief in February and March, and between 9 and 11 per cent. in the three following months. Next came the Darbhanga district with a ratio of between 10 and 12 per cent. in May and June. These are the two districts in Behar in which distress was most severe, and there is evidence that owing to the smallness of the tenants' holdings, the poverty of much of the soil, the malarial character of the climate and the dense population, the people of the Champaran district are particularly poor and depressed. In Punjab, over 10 per cent. of the population of the Hissar district were on relief from the middle of February to the middle of July, and over 12 per cent. in June. In the North-Western Provinces and Oudh, the Bundelkhand districts, where intense famine prevailed, naturally exhibit the highest percentages. In the Banda district, over 31 per cent. of a population of 705,000 were in receipt of relief from February to June. In the Jalaun district 25 per cent. were on relief during the same period. In Hamirpur and Jhansi, 16 per cent. were on relief, and in Allahabad 19 per cent. In Oudh, relief was given for six months to 11 per cent. of the population of the Hardoi district. These represent the extreme cases in the North-Western Provinces and Oudh. In other districts in those provinces, the proportion of relief rarely exceeded 3 or 4 per cent. of the total population. The magnitude of the relief given in the Bundelkhand districts of the North-Western Provinces and Oudh was surpassed in the distressed districts of the Madras Deccan in June, July and August this year. In the Kurnool and Bellary districts from 30 to 40 per cent. of the population were in receipt of relief during those three months, and in the Anantapur district 29 per cent. As famine was not intense in in these parts, there can be little doubt that the easy terms on which relief was offered attracted persons who would have refused relief under more exacting conditions. Compared with the Madras figures the ratios of relief in the Deccan districts of the Bombay Presidency were comparatively low. The highest rates were attained in the districts of Bijapur and Sholapur, where for some months 10 to 12 per cent. of the population were on relief. In August the ratio in Bijapur rose to 16 per cent., and for a few days in September to 20 per cent. In Ahmednagar also 10 per cent. of the population were on relief in February and March, and again in July and August. In the other districts in the Bombay Deccan the proportion was much lower. In the Central Provinces the highest ratios were attained in some districts in May and June before the rains broke, but in others not until the last months of the famine. With the setting in of the rains the numbers on relief works greatly decreased, and in districts where the numbers on the works had been large the decrease under this head of relief was not made good by the expansion of gratuitous relief during the rains. In the table in the margin, which gives the percentages of relief in different months in the twelve most distressed districts of the Central Provinces, the two Nerbudda valley districts of Hoshangabad and Narsinghpur, the Saugor district and the Raipur district are instances in point. In these districts the relief-work population up to the rains was exceptionally large. The numbers on the works in these districts declined rapidly when the rains set in, and although gratuitous relief has in these districts been since expanded, the expansion has not made good the fall in the number of relief workers. On the other hand, the Betul, Seoni and Bilaspur districts are instances of the great increase in gratuitous relief and children's kitchens which in the latter months of the famine has been forced upon the authorities by the special circumstances of the season, and the condition of certain classes of the people.

Percentage of population on relief at the end of—

—	May.	June.	July.	August.	September.
Saugor ...	10	6	6	6	6
Damoh ...	14	13	14	23	10
Jabalpur ...	16	10	15	13	13
Mandla ...	10	5	5	10	10
Seoni ...	8	5	5	9	17
Narsinghpur	14	6	8	9	7
Hoshangabad	17	8	13	11	9
Betul ...	13	7	9	11	18
Chhindwara	10	10	11	10	13
Balaghat ...	16	11	14	13	11
Raipur ...	15	9	9	10	12
Bilaspur ...	6	7	10	11	13

The cost of relief per head.

99. A convenient method of stating the total quantity of relief given in a province or district is to express it in the form of relief units of one day each. Thus a person who is relieved throughout a month of 30 days counts as 30 units. By

adopting this method the volume and cost of relief in each Province can be readily compared. In Appendix V the number of relief units relieved from October 1896 to September 1897 is shown to be 800 millions, or excluding Berar, which is administered under special conditions, 796 millions. The direct expenditure on relief in British India (excluding Berar) has been shown to approximately amount to 680 lakhs of rupees up to the end of September 1897. The average cost per relief unit, that is, of one day's relief for each person, works out to ·085 of a rupee, or little over $1\frac{1}{3}$ annas.* As this includes expenditure on tools and plant and on establishment, in addition to the actual sums spent on relief, the scale of relief seems extremely low, especially in a year when an anna would buy but $1\frac{1}{2}$ or $1\frac{1}{4}$ lbs. of coarse grain, and sometimes not that. But it has to be remembered that relief has been given to every member of a family in want, down to the infant in arms, that about 25 per cent. of the relief units were children, and that the relief wages and doles were regulated with the knowledge that in many places the people were not at the end of their resources. Low as the cost has been in British India as a whole, in particular provinces it was even lower. The lowest rate was reached in Bengal and in the North-Western Provinces and Oudh. The rate in the latter provinces is equivalent to 1·12 annas per unit. The highest rate was found in Burma, which is due to relief being chiefly given there in the form of wages to relief workers, most of whom were able-bodied persons doing a good task and earning a substantial wage. The high rate in the Central Provinces is probably due to the very high prices which have continuously maintained there, and which have necessitated a correspondingly high scale of money payments.

—	Millions of relief units.	Expenditure on relief.	Cost per relief unit.
		Rs.	Rs.
Madras	92	90,00,000	·098
Bombay	11	1,11,00,000	·098
Bengal	139	1,13,00,000	·080
North-Western Provinces and Oudh.	284	1,95,00,000	·070
Punjab	21	18,00,000	·036
Central Provinces	138	1,41,00,000	·103
Burma	8	11,00,000	·139

XI.—*The grain trade and the railways.*

The weekly return of grain imports and exports.

100. Among the measures which were taken by the Government of India in the late famine for obtaining and publishing information as to the course of the grain trade throughout the country was one which is believed to have proved of considerable public utility. Arrangements were made in each district by which the district officer at the end of each week received a return from each railway station in his district of the imports and exports of grain during the week. These returns were totalled up for the district and communicated to the Statistical Bureau in Calcutta, which collated and published them week by week for the whole of India. Anyone studying these returns could form a good idea of what each district was doing in the matter of importing or exporting grain, and this information proved valuable both to the trade and to the Government. In Appendix VII to this Narrative a summary of the statistical information thus collated is given. It soon became apparent from the weekly returns that although the grain trade was active and alert, and the movements of grain throughout India considerable, there was not that vast drain of food from one province to meet the necessities of another that marked the famine of 1876–78. In the great Southern India famine of 1876–78 the railways were taxed beyond their carrying capacity to feed the population of Madras, Mysore and Bombay. Grain lay for weeks at railway stations and in goods sheds all over the country waiting for carriage, and this notwithstanding the precedence which had been given on the railways to grain consigned to the famine districts over all other classes of traffic. In 1876–78 the Madras Railway carried nearly 1,000,000 tons of grain, and the South Indian Railway nearly 400,000 tons, into the

* When the exchange value of the rupee is 16 pence, the anna is equivalent to a penny. At the present moment the exchange value of the rupee is $15\frac{3}{4}$ pence.

distressed districts of Madras. During the same period the railways carried 267,000 tons of grain into the distressed districts of the Bombay Deccan and 166,000 tons were conveyed into them by carts up the ghâts from the small ports on the coast. At no time during the late famine has there been excessive pressure on the railways. This in itself is not a conclusive fact in the comparison, as the carrying power of the Indian railways to any one point is probably quite double what it was in 1876-78. But at no time during the present year has the grain-trade been in an excited state, nor so far as at present an opinion can be formed in the absence of the complete railway returns for the months in question, has the traffic in grain approached in volume that of 1876-78. The explanation seems to be that, owing to the wide area affected by the drought, there was no province in a position of such security as to be able to let very much of its surplus go. Prices throughout India were nearly on the same level, and markets were too sensitive for very large and continuous exports or imports. Most of the distressed districts also seem to have had considerable reserves of food stocks at the beginning of the famine, which were drawn upon as required. This was eminently the case in the Central Provinces. The largest import into any district in those provinces

Amount of grain imports into certain districts.

from January 1897 to September was 17,300 tons into Nagpur. This represents nine months' food for about 140,000 persons, the population of the district being 758,000. In other districts which were much more distressed than Nagpur, the imports of food were considerably smaller. Saugor imported 12,000 tons during the period covered by the returns and Bhandara 10,700 tons. On the other hand, Raipur and Sambalpur exported large quantities of rice, the nett export being 22,600 tons from Sambalpur and 14,000 tons from Bilaspur. In Bengal the imports into certain districts were on a larger scale. Darbhanga stands first with a nett import from January to September of 44,500 tons, followed by Saran with 44,100 tons and by Muzaffapur with 32,900 tons. These imports were chiefly Burma rice from Calcutta. Other Bengal districts exported largely, notably Burdwan (60,958 tons), Birbhum (59,308 tons), Midnapur (39,503 tons), and Balasore (42,821 tons). It is not known to what places these exports chiefly went, but possibly a good deal was taken by Calcutta. In the North-Western Provinces and Oudh the districts in which distress was most intense show, as might be expected, the largest importations, Allahabad having a nett import of 45,529 tons, Banda of 23,573 tons and Jhansi of 17,123 tons. The Meerut Division, as might also be expected, exported considerable quantities. In the Punjab the Hissar district imported 35,985 tons, a quantity sufficient to feed for nine months more than one-third of the population of the district. Some of the Punjab districts exported largely, especially those of the Jalundhar Divisions. The Deccan districts of Bombay all show considerable imports. Poona importing 38,700 tons, Khandesh 37,800 tons. Bijapur 25,500 tons and Satara 21,900 tons. But as above remarked, these imports, though large, are not on the scale of the imports of 1876-78. The case of Bijapur is a good illustration of the extent to which old stocks of grain must have existed in this part of the country at the beginning of the drought. This district, though it practically had no crops at all in 1896-97, was able to get through the famine with an import which represented food for about one-fourth only of the population. Of this import, more than half occurred during the last three months of the famine, indicating that local reserves of food were by that time on the point of exhaustion. Had not rain opportunely fallen in September 1897, the grain imports into the Bombay Deccan would in all probability have risen to very great dimensions. The distressed districts of the Madras Deccan imported comparatively little grain from outside. The nett import from January to September into Bellary was 16,900 tons, of which 10,700 tons were imported in the last three months. Kurnool imported only 3,400 tons. Anantapur and Cuddapah show a small nett export. On the other hand, some of the Madras districts show very large exports, notably the Tanjore district (143,000 tons), the Godavery district (53,000 tons), the Kistna district (43,300 tons), and the South Arcot district (35,800 tons). Much of this grain, it is believed, went to the Bombay Presidency, where prices have ruled continuously higher than in Madras. There is little doubt that owing to good harvests generally in 1895-96, and to good harvests in the southern districts in 1896-97, the Madras Presidency at the beginning of the famine held large stocks of grain in excess of its requirements, and that the richer districts must have done very well in disposing of their surplus at very high prices. But for the distress prevailing outside its boundaries, and the consequent demand for grain throughout India, very low prices must have prevailed this year throughout the Madras Presidency.

The great service rendered by the railways.

101. No occasion has thus arisen during the late famine for the railways to exhibit their carrying capacity to its full extent. Still the grain traffic dealt with by them so quietly and easily was infinitely greater than could have been disposed of by country carts and cattle, the sources of supply were infinitely enlarged through the virtual annihilation of distance as an obstacle to profitable trade and the cost and burden of transport was infinitely lessened. In many parts of India, especially the Deccan and Central India and the Punjab, the absence of water and fodder in a famine year makes carriage of grain by road for long distances almost impossible. Apart from the service actually rendered by the railways, the fact of their being there, and the knowledge of their great potential carrying power, have been of incalculable value. Though the railway imports of grain into Bijapur or Banda represented food for only one-fourth or one-third of the population of those districts, it was known that the import could be easily doubled at any time if the local demand required it. This knowledge gave complete confidence both to officials and to the public at large. Had Bijapur or Banda not been connected by railway communication with other marts, all the difficulties about food supplies which in such places have troubled the administration in past famines would assuredly have arisen this year in a most acute form. In 1877 grain had to be sent by the Bombay Government by cart to Bijapur as "the tract was so distant and difficult of access." In 1870 the Government of the North-Western Provinces and Oudh had to make similar importations into Bundelkhand to allay panic. These are two cases out of many in which, since the Famine Commission reported in 1881, railway communication has been given to remote districts liable to famine. What is true of Banda is equally true of the other districts in British Bundelkhand, and of the native states of Central India forming the Bundelkhand and Bagelkhand Agencies, and served by the Indian Midland Railway and its branches. What is true of Bijapur is equally true of Belgaum, Dharwar and the rest of the Deccan country traversed by the Southern Mahratta Railway. It is indeed difficult to realise the extent to which the task of famine relief has been simplified and facilitated over vast areas of India by the extension given to railways during the last fifteen years.

The railways recommended by the Famine Commission have been made.

102. The Famine Commission saw that in the extension of railways lay the hope of improving the conditions under which the famine administrator had to do his work. It may be well to show in this place what has been done to carry out the recommendations of the Famine Commission in the matter. The Famine Commission found about 9,000 miles of open railway in India, and they came to the conclusion that the country would be adequately protected as to communications by the addition of about 10,000 miles to the existing mileage. In December 1896, over 20,000 miles of railway were open. The Famine Commission's wish has thus been more than fulfilled. Not only that, all the lines which they especially recommended for the purposes of famine protection, have, with one exception—the East Coast Railway, been made, and the line which form the exception is now in course of completion. The tracts which they singled out as specially deficient in railway communication comprised North Behar, the Bundelkhand districts of the North-Western Provinces, the southern Punjab and the southern Mahratta country of Bombay. They also drew attention to the advantages which would result from direct communication between the rich deltas of the Godavery and Kishna districts and the Madras Deccan, and between Orissa and Bengal. A glance at the modern railway map of India will show that these recommendations have been fully met. Not only north Behar, but also northern Oudh, have been thoroughly opened up by the Bengal and North-Western Railway system and its Tirhoot branches. The value of this system

has been abundantly proved in the late famine in Behar. The Bundelkhand districts of the North-Western Provinces and a large part of Central India are now traversed by the Indian Midland from Jhansi to Itarsi, with a most valuable famine protective cross-line from Jhansi to Agra on one side, and from Jhansi to Banda, and the East Indian Railway on the other. This railway has been the salvation this year of British and Native Bundelkhand. The south-eastern districts of the Punjab have been brought into direct communication with the large grain-emporia of the North-Western Provinces and the Punjab, by the Rewari-Ferozepur line. On this line the Hissar district has depended this year for its food. In Bombay two branches of the Southern Mahratta Railway intersect the worst districts of the Deccan and southern Mahratta country from north to south, while the same system connects them with Mysore on the south, and with Madras, through Bellary and Kurnool, to the Kishna and the Godavery districts on the east. Until this system was constructed, this tract of country was more insecure and liable to dearth than any other part of British India. Now the surplus produce of the rich delta districts of Madras can now find its way into all parts of the Madras and the Bombay Deccan, and in the late famine this facility has been largely used. The East Coast Railway from Bezwada on the Kishna river to Cuttack in Orissa, and thence north to Midnapur and Calcutta will complete the programme which the Famine Commission had in view. There is still another large railway system to be mentioned which was not within their purview, but which has proved of inestimable value to the Central Provinces in the late famine. The Bengal-Nagpur line, starting from Nagpur on the Great Indian Peninsula line, and terminating at Asansol on the East Indian Railway, traverses in its course of 600 miles the great rice-plain of Chhattisgarh, and has brought this once remote and inaccessible country into connection with Bengal on the one side and Bombay on the other. An important branch from Bilaspur in Chhattisgarh to Katni on the East Indian Railway line, running from Allahabad to Jubbulpur, also links the Chhattisgarh plain with Upper India. In the late famine great stores of rice found their way by this railway system from Sambalpur and Raipur to many distressed districts in and outside the Central Provinces, and by the same route came 50,000 tons of Burma rice from Calcutta to Bilaspur and other distressed districts in the provinces. This railway has also been invaluable in other ways to the Local Government in its administration of the famine. Without it the head of the province would at its provincial head-quarters at Nagpur have been separated by over two hundred miles of road from the centre of the Chhattisgarh Division, and at such a distance effective supervision becomes very difficult. The still existing defects of railway communication in many parts of the Central Provinces, and the difficult character of much of the country, have, as it is, made famine administration in this part of India exceptionally arduous. That the task would have been very much greater had the Bengal-Nagpur Railway not been in existence, is obvious to anyone observing the place it fills in the map of the province. The present most pressing want of the provinces in the matter of further railway protection is a line to traverse in one or more directions the oblong block of country enclosed by the existing systems of the Great Indian Peninsula Railway and the Bengal-Nagpur Railway. This oblong comprises a tangled mass of hills and upland plain, and amid these Satpura hills are situate districts such as Seoni, Betul, Mandla, Balaghat and Chhindwara, which have suffered much in the late famine and have given cause for continuous anxiety. Communication between them and the surrounding lowlands is at present conducted by means of roads with necessarily steep gradients, which tell heavily on the weak bullock carriage of the country, and which are consequently at all times serious obstacles to the trader, and in the rainy months almost prohibitive of traffic. Proposals have been made for a system of light railways to open up this country to protect it against a similar famine and to give it a market for its surplus produce in good years. These proposals, however, are still in the tentative stage, as very careful inquiry will be required before any decision can be pronounced on the engineering and financial difficulties with which the project is surrounded.

XII.—*Irrigation and the Famine.*

Irrigation in 1877.

103. As the extension of railways tends to lessen the acuteness of a famine, so the extension of works of irrigation tends to prevent it. The extent to which effect has been given to the recommendations of the Famine Commission in the matter of railway communications has been described. It remains to notice briefly what has been done to carry out the equally important recommendations made by that body with regard to the improvement and extension of works of irrigation. The Famine Commission found that of the 192 millions of acres cultivated in British India, about 28½ millions were irrigated, of which 7½ million acres were irrigated by canals, and the rest from wells, tanks, running streams and the like.*

* *Area ordinarily irrigated in 1877.*

Province.	Canals.	Wells.	Tanks, streams, etc.	Total.
Punjab	1,670,000	3,200,000	630,000	5,500,000
North-Western Provinces and Oudh.	1,700,000	5,800,000	400,000	11,500,000
Bengal	360,000	600,000	40,000	1,000,000
Central Provinces ...	*Nil.*	120,000	650,000	770,000
Berar	*Nil.*	*Nil.*	100,000	100,000
Bombay	25,000	425,000		450,000
Sind	1,800,000	*Nil.*	*Nil.*	1,800,000
Madras	2,000,000	2 300.000	3.000.000	7,300,000
Total	7,555,000	20,865,000		28,420,000

104. These figures were only approximately correct, especially as regards irrigation from wells and tanks. The area shown as irrigated from these sources in the North-Western Provinces and Oudh seems in excess of the actual facts. In the case of Sind the area under "canals" included private inundation canals as well as Government works. In the case of the Punjab the "canal" area included small inundation canals of a temporary character, which are now classed as "minor works for which no capital accounts are kept." Making deductions on account of these, the area irrigated from State irrigation works of a permanent character in 1877 cannot be put higher than 7 millions of acres. In the case of Madras no returns were available for the large zemindari estates, and even in respect of Government lands the area irrigated by wells had to be guessed at. The figures given for well and tank irrigation in Bengal were also largely based on assumptions. The difficulties which the Famine Commission experienced in arriving at an accurate statement of the acreage protected by irrigation still exist. It can, however, be shown that under the head of "canal" irrigation a great advance has been made, and that the irrigation from wells and "other sources" has also extended in many provinces.

The recommendations of the Famine Commission.

105. The recommendations of the Famine Commission related chiefly to canal irrigation, including in this term not only irrigation from rivers, but also irrigation from large storage reservoirs or tanks, in which the drainage of the surrounding country is caught and retained. Dealing first with the province of the Punjab, they urged the necessity for giving greater protection to the arid country between the Jumna and the Sutlej rivers by enlarging the Western Jumna canal and by completing the Sirhind canal on the east bank of the Sutlej. They further recommended the gradual extension of irrigation canals in the waste and waterless plains between the Sutlej and the Chenab, and between the Chenab and Jhelum rivers. All these recommendations have been acted on. The Western Jumna Canal has been remodelled and enlarged to provide water for the Sirsa branch, which gives irrigation to parts of the Hissar and Karnal districts. The Sirhind Canal was completed in 1887 at a cost of nearly Rx. 2,300,000, and irrigates between 800,000 and 900,000 acres. The Chenab Canal, between the Sutlej and the Chenab, will cost about the same sum. Though still an incomplete work, it has already enabled 500,000 acres of virgin soil to be brought under tillage, and it will, when complete, irrigate over a million acres. The agricultural

The Punjab.

colonies on this canal are one of the happiest experiments of reclamation of waste which have been essayed in India. The value of the crops on this canal this year may, at a very moderate estimate, be put at Rx. 2,100,000. In addition to these large works, several smaller canals have been constructed since the Famine Commission wrote, notably the Swat River Canal, at a cost of Rx. 363,000, and the Sidhnai Canal, and considerable sums have been expended on improving the Bari-Doab Canal and the minor inundation canals on the Indus and the Sutlej. The total capital expenditure on irrigation works in the Punjab, for which capital and revenue accounts are kept, now amounts to Rx. 7,800,000. In 1895-96 the area irrigated by these works amounted to 3,150,000 acres. In 1896–97, under the stimulus of the drought, the area irrigated from these works in the Punjab was 3,900,000 acres. Nearly 300,000 acres in addition were irrigated from inundation canals from the Indus, which are classed as "works for which no capital accounts are kept." According to a return made by the Agricultural Department, the total crop area of the Punjab in 1896–97 was 18 millions of acres, of which 8,200,000 acres, or 47 per cent., were irrigated. Canals irrigated 4,198,000 acres, wells fed from canals 413,000 acres, and wells and ponds 4,203,000 acres. When it is further remembered that the crops on unirrigated lands were very poor, while the crops on irrigated lands were generally very good, some idea may be formed of the value of irrigation to the Punjab in a year of drought.

The North-Western Provinces and Oudh.

106. In the North-Western Provinces and Oudh the completion of the Lower Ganges Canal, the construction of a canal on the Betwa river in the Jhansi district as a protective work for Bundelkhand, and the further investigation of the Sarda Canal project for Oudh, were recommended by the Famine Commission. The first two recommendations have been carried out. The Lower Ganges Canal has added, at a capital cost of Rx. 3,200,000, one million acres to the irrigable canal area of the province. The Betwa Canal, which was executed at a cost of Rx. 400,000 charged to the Famine Insurance Fund, is capable of irrigating about 100,000 acres, and this year it has irrigated 85,000 acres. But in ordinary years, owing to the peculiarity of the predominant soils and the prejudices of the cultivators, the demand for water on this canal is disappointingly small. The Sarda Canal project is still under investigation, and it is still doubtful whether a canal would prove beneficial or remunerative in a tract like Oudh, where the rainfall is ordinarily sufficient and where irrigation from wells and tanks is extensively practised. The total capital expenditure on major and minor irrigation works in the North-Western Provinces and Oudh now amounts to Rx. 8,000,000, and in 1895–6 the area irrigated from them was 2,100,000 acres. In 1896–97 this rose to 3,100,000 acres. According to the returns of the Agricultural Department the total area cropped in the North-Western Provinces and Oudh in 1896-97 was 36¼ million acres, against an average of nearly 42 million acres. About 12,000,000 acres, or 33 per cent. of the total, were irrigated. This province, like the Punjab, would have fared very badly in the late drought but for its irrigation, and like the Punjab its canal irrigation has largely increased since 1877, while the area irrigated by wells and tanks has certainly not decreased.

Bengal.

107. With regard to Bengal the Famine Commission, while admitting that Orissa canals had been anything but a success, were of opinion that an additional Rx. 400,000 would be well spent in raising the irrigable area from 183,000 acres to 500,000. They also recommended the investigation of certain projects for canals from the Gandak river in North Behar. Their recommendation as to the Orissa canals has been given effect to, and the total capital outlay on this system, which was Rx. 1,750,000 when they wrote, now exceeds Rx. 2,500,000. But the irrigated area in no year exceeds 180,000 acres, and in most years falls below 150,000 acres. The canals do not pay their working expenses, and continue to be an example of irrigation in a wrong place. On the Sone canals in Behar considerable sums have been spent since 1877, as the capital outlay has risen from Rx. 1,900,000 to Rx. 2,600,000. The irrigated area from these works now averages about 400,000 acres, but in years of drought reaches 550,000 acres. The total capital outlay on major and minor irrigation works in Bengal exceeds Rx. 6,000,000, on which the interest charge

amounts to Rx. 239,000 a year, to meet which the nett revenue is only Rx. 12,000. The direct financial results of irrigation in Bengal are therefore disappointing.

Bombay.

108. This was also acknowledged by the Famine Commission to be the case in Bombay. The outlay on irrigation works in that Presidency amounted to Rx. 1,280,000 in 1877, while the area irrigated was only 25,000 acres. The outlay on major works has now risen to Rx. 1,800,000, but the irrigated area rarely exceeds 60,000 acres, and the nett revenue is quite insufficient to meet the charges on account of interest. On minor irrigation works for which capital accounts are kept, and which irrigate about 26,000 acres, there is a further outlay of Rx. 650,000. Irrigation from State works thus shows no great advance in the Deccan or Gujerat since 1877. Referring to the disappointing results of the irrigation canals in the Sholapur district the Director of Agriculture in March last stated that the supply of water from the catchment areas must, from the first, have been largely over estimated. Always insufficient, it diminishes greatly in dry years. He admitted, however, that indirectly these reservoirs contribute to the irrigation of a larger area than is recorded against them, by improving the water-supply of wells beneath them. The same authority showed that since 1877 the progress in well irrigation has been considerable. In Sholapur, Ahmadnagar and Satara this year over 100,000 acres in each district were thus protected, in Poona 75,000 acres and in Nasik 60,000 acres. The loans made by the Government for wells in the present year have given a great stimulus to this movement, and everywhere in the course of his tour the Director was surprised at the activity shown in the repair and the construction of wells by the people.

Sindh.

109. With regard to Sindh the recommendation of the Famine Commission that the system of inundation canals from the Indus should be extended and improved has been fully carried out. The area irrigated by major and minor State works for which capital and revenue accounts are kept exceeds 1,200,000 acres ; and there is a nett revenue of Rx. 100,000 on a capital outlay of Rx. 1,450,000. A further area of 1,100,000 acres is irrigated from minor works for which capital accounts are not kept, and which yield a nett revenue of Rx. 128,000. The total State irrigation in Sindh averages about 2,300,000 acres, which is a considerable increase on the figures of 1877.

Madras.

110. The chief recommendations made by the Famine Commission with regard to Madras were that the important and highly remunerative canals in the deltas of the Godavery, Kishna and Caveri should be completed, and that the Periyar irrigation project for providing water for nearly 200,000 acres in the Madura district should be undertaken. They also recommended for consideration the Sangam anicut system, which was calculated to irrigate 77,000 acres in the Nellore district, and the Rushikuliya project in the Ganjam district. On the completion of the three great deltaic systems about Rx. 1,100,000 has been spent since 1877, and the irrigation from them has increased from 1,600,000 acres to 2,200,000 acres. The Sangam anicut system has been completed at the cost of Rx. 310,000. The Periyar project is on the eve of completion at the cost of Rx. 850,000, and the Rushikulya project, which will cost Rx. 440,000, is in progress. The total capital outlay on major irrigation works in the Madras Presidency is nearly Rx. 6,500,000, they irrigate an area of 2,700,000 acres, they have a nett revenue of Rx. 472,000 (excluding a nett revenue of Rx. 360,000 due to old irrigation which is not represented in the capital accounts), and they earn over 7 per cent. on the capital outlay. A further area of 535,000 acres is irrigated from minor works for which capital accounts are kept, and a further area of 3,234,633 acres from minor works, chiefly small tanks, for which capital accounts are not kept. This gives a total area of 6½ millions of acres of irrigation under State supervision in the Presidency.

111. Summing up the progress made in State irrigation since 1877, it may be said that the capital outlay on works for which capital accounts are kept has increased from Rx. 20,000,000 to Rx. 35,000,000, the gross revenue from

Rx. 1,688,000 to Rx. 3,100,000, and the area irrigated from 7 millions of acres to 10 millions of acres. In addition, from 4½ to 5 millions of acres are irrigated from small State works, for which no capital accounts are kept.

XIII.—The Indian Famine Charitable Relief Fund.

112. The operations of the Indian Famine Charitable Relief Fund do not come within the scope of this narrative, but no account of the famine of 1896–97 would be complete which omitted mention of this most signal and beneficent manifestation of national benevolence. The sentiments of gratitude and appreciation evoked in India by this great tribute of England's charity have been vividly described by those charged with its distribution. Here it may be permissible to dwell on the almost incalculable value of the Fund as an agency in alleviating human suffering, and in restoring thousands of ruined agriculturists to their place in society. The responsibilities accepted by the State in India in a time of famine are very great. It undertakes to keep the people alive, and it helps them by loans and advances and suspensions and remissions of land revenue to return to their usual vocations and to retrieve their fortunes, when the calamity has passed. But it does not undertake to prevent all suffering or privation or to replace in each individual case the resources exhausted by famine. In duty to the tax-payer it is also obliged to surround the offer of relief with certain conditions and self-acting tests of distress, to rigidly limit the amount of relief given to the minimum necessary to sustain life and health, and to withhold relief from those who, though they may suffer, are not in patent distress, and who refrain through feelings of pride, or caste or family prejudices, to apply for work or to appear at a public kitchen. There is thus wide scope for the legitimate exercise of private benevolence which, without pauperising or demoralising the people or relieving the State of its accepted obligations, will fill up the inevitable gaps in any State scheme of relief, and lighten the long train of indirect ills with which the State in its struggle with famine does not profess to deal. The presence or absence of such charity, organised on methodical principles and working in conjunction with the official system of relief, makes a world of difference to the afflicted population, and may vitally determine the degree of rapidity and completeness with which it shakes off the effect of the calamity, and returns to normal conditions of well-being. The magnitude of the resources placed by the public benevolence on this occasion at the disposal of the Indian Famine Charitable Relief Fund Association has enabled this great work of restoration to be carried out on a very extensive scale. According to the latest financial return issued by the Executive Committee appointed to administer the fund, they have had the disposal of Rx. 1,646,000 in cash, besides large gifts of grain and clothing. Of this sum, upwards of £765,000, which yielded on being remitted to India Rx. 1,225,000, has been received from the United Kingdom, Rx. 136,000 from English colonies and dependencies and foreign countries, and Rx. 285,000 from India itself. Elsewhere it has been shown in the narrative that the direct expenditure by the Indian Government on famine relief up to the end of September amounts to Rx. 6,800,000. The Famine Fund has distributed in charitable relief a sum equivalent to nearly one-fourth of the direct expenditure incurred by the State. If it be remembered that the bounty of the Fund has in no wise displaced relief which otherwise would have been given by the State, that the State relief has not been confined within pre-determined financial bounds and has been limited only by the enforcement of certain conditions and tests, mostly of the self-acting order, some idea may be formed of the effect which this great independent stream of charity has had in softening the sharpness of distress and restoring countless humble households to comparative prosperity. The financial accounts of the Fund are at present incomplete, but so far as a judgment may be formed from the details of the expenditure which has so far been returned, it would seem that fully three-fourths of the Fund will be spent in "restoring to their original position those who have lost their all in the struggle, and in giving them a fresh start in life." Gifts of seed and cattle to the cultivator, gifts of tools and raw material to the artizan, gifts for the repair of ruined houses and the replacement of household requisites, gifts to keep the family from want until the

crops on the ground ripen, these are some of the most obvious ways in which this object has been effected. From all quarters overwhelming evidence pours in of the inestimable benefits conferred by bounty directed to this end, and of its recuperative effect on people whose spirits have been depressed and whose energies have been dulled by long continued misfortunes. If, as may be hoped, the stress of famine is now passing away and prosperity returning to the land, one of the most potent instruments to this much wished for consummation will be the Indian Famine Charitable Relief Fund of 1896-97. The renewed prosperity of India will constitute an abiding memorial of the large-hearted benevolence and sympathy which called that Fund into being, and made it what it was.

The 15th October, 1897.
SIMLA.

Malarial Fever in the Central Provinces (see foot-note to page 50 of Narrative).

1. *Extract from letter of Chief Commissioner, Central Provinces, No. 1948–F., dated 15th October, 1897.*

The month of September is in these Provinces always recognized, with August and October, as the most unhealthy season of the year, and a large increase of mortality is usually to be expected in this month. The figures for September are not yet available, but from such indications as may be gathered from the reports and from the weekly returns it may be hoped that, although in some districts, and those not the most severely distressed, the death-rates have again risen, there will prove to have been, on the whole, a sensible diminution of the terribly high rate reached in August. The rates given in the Commissioner's memorandum for the Jubbulpore Division show a very marked decrease in Mandla and Seoni, where the mortality in August was exceptionally high, and a slight increase in only one district, Jubbulpore, where the August rate was, considering the conditions of the year, remarkably low. If these anticipations are confirmed by the special mortality return now under preparation, it may safely be said that the worst is now over, and that a rapid return to normal rates of mortality may be hoped for. There is no doubt from the observations made by officers who enquired personally and locally into the high mortality of August and September, that the bulk of it was due to fever, which attacked alike the poor and the well-to-do,—those who suffered from privation and those who did not. The Commissioner of Jubbulpore describes, in paragraph 12 of his memorandum, the effect of the "wave of malignant fever" which swept over Saugor. The account given by the Deputy Commissioner of Chhindwara (paragraph 7 of the Nerbudda memorandum) of the result of his personal enquiries in the Sausar Tahsil of that district point to a similar condition of things there. And reports to the same effect come from other districts also. Thus the Deputy Commissioner of Hoshangabad writes :—

"Fever this year is unusually prevalent, and no house is free from it. * * * The main peculiarity in the mortality is the high proportion of deaths among children five and over, and persons fifty and over. * * * Harda I have not seen since the beginning of September, but in my tour in that tahsil I came across several recent deaths in really wealthy families."

And the Deputy Commissioner of Jubbulpore writes :—

"The unhealthy character of the season has greatly to do with the rise in mortality. Fevers are extremely prevalent in every quarter of the district."

A further proof of the unhealthiness of the season is to be found in the deplorable amount of sickness among the famine-relief staff. Officers of all grades have been repeatedly incapacitated by fever, and two—Lieutenant Hamilton Moore in Bilaspur, and Naib-Tahsildar Mukund Ram in Seoni—have died from illness contracted during their inspections. Both these officers, in their several capacities, had been doing excellent work, and both fell victims to their devotion to duty. The Chief Commissioner greatly regrets their loss.

---

2. *Extract from Famine Report for September* 1897 *of the Committee of the Jubbulpore Division.*

The portentous increase in the death-rates of Saugor, Mandla and Seoni during the month of August was noticed in last month's report. It remains to accentuate the fact that during that month fever attacked certain tracts with pestilential severity. From some points of view the increase in the Saugor death-rate was one of the most unsatisfactory features of the month, as there were no such difficulties to be encountered in this district as in the wilds of Mandla and Seoni, and famine relief should have been as efficient as in Damoh or Jubbulpore. I have lately spent twelve days touring in the interior of the Saugor district and have made detailed enquiries into the mortality of the villages I came across. The general results have been separately reported, but I may note here that they indicated that a wave of malignant fever passed across the district such as was experienced in some districts of the North-Western Provinces after the famine of 1877, and that, as in the North-Western Provinces on that occasion, the well-to-do suffered equally with the poor. On the occasion of my visit to Saugor I was assured that not a household in the city have escaped sickness. Of 45 clerks in the Deputy Commissioner's office, 11 had been incapacitated for duty in August and 10 in September, for periods which gave an average of a week to each man. At one time sickness deprived the Executive Engineer of the services of seven out of his nine clerks. The police force suffered from an abnormal amount of sickness, 13·4 per cent. of the strength being in hospital during August, and numbers being invalided at their homes from lack of hospital accommodation. Similar reports, though not in so much detail, have reached me from Mandla and Seoni, and it may be accepted that a very large proportion of the abnormal mortality of August resulted from sickness which, so far as one can judge, was quite unconnected with the scarcity of food, and may have proceeded from the rise in the water level from the abnormal depth to which it had fallen through the long period of drought.

---

3. *Extract from Famine Memorandum for September* 1897 *of the Commissioner of the Nerbudda Division.*

We must turn to districts whose administrative officers are less chary of utterance in order to get the fuller information which we require. In the adjoining district of Chhindwara (and especially in the Sausar Tahsil) the conditions as to climate, etc., are somewhat similar to those of Betul. Mr. Ryves records that, finding the mortality in the Sausar Tahsil running up during September to an extent which made a death-rate of 123 per mille per annum probable, he personally visited the tahsil and examined the registers of the Sausar Station-house, and of the two outposts at Ranakona and Mohgaon, and endeavoured to ascertain the causes of the mortality by checking the deaths of one or two villages on the spot. He gives the results of his enquiry in the following words :—

"The population of the Police-posts inspected is 40,122, and the mortality reported during September 357, giving a death-rate of 106·8 per 1,000 per annum, but in the Mohgaon Outpost Circle it was as high as 147 per cent. This mortality classified according to the ages of the deceased was as follows :—

Age.	No. of deaths.
0— 1 years ...	53
1— 5 „ ...	53
5—10 „ ...	15
10—15 „ ...	18
15—20 „ ...	7
20—30 „ ...	26
30—40 „ ...	17
40—50 „ ...	38
50—60 „ ...	31
Over 60 „ ...	99

"It will be observed that very nearly half the deaths occurred among infants under 1 year of age and among aged people over 60 years of age.

The causes of death were as follows :—

	No.
Fever ...	236
Dysentery ...	34
Other Causes ...	81
Small-pox ...	2
Accident ...	2

"It will be noticed that diarrhœa and dysentery, which have been the most fertile causes of death in poor-houses and famine hospitals, play quite a minor part compared to malarial fever. 'Other causes' include lung affections of all descriptions not classed as fever.

"The heaviest mortality in the Mohgaon Circle occurred in the large village of Pipla Narsinwar. Here 36 deaths occurred in a population of 3,288, giving a percentage of 130 per thousand per annum. I visited this village and checked the kotwal's register of deaths. I found that the malguzar of this place had for some months been distributing grain to the poor, and that six deaths were those of wandering beggars, who had come to the village attracted by this fact. The deaths among residents had occurred among the well-to-do classes with as much frequency as among the poor. The death-roll, for instance, included two Marwaris, a well-to do Brahmin, a Sunar and five or six Telis, all of them persons in good circumstances, and further enquiries into the deaths among the lower classes failed to elicit one in which privation could be said to have been the determining cause. The malguzas, Ganpat Singh, had in fact taken measures which precluded that supposition. In other villages, namely, Singhpur, Koparwari, Ridhora, Jokiwara and Jam, I made similar enquiries and found that the deaths in these villages were equally divided between rich and poor.

"To turn to the Chhindwara Tahsil, the Mokher outpost area, with a population 13,118, has a mortality of 189, giving a death-rate of 168 per thousand per annum. In this area Mauza Ekulbehri headed the list with a population of 1,186 and a death-roll of 18. I visited this village, and made a house-to-house inspection, and found it to contain only one man showing signs of emaciation, He was by no means in bad case, and had been in receipt of relief for more than a month. Nine people were in receipt of relief, of whom two had asked to have their names struck off as they were able to provide for themselves, and did not wish to be classed as "kangals" (*i.e.*, destitute persons) longer than was necessary. Examining the register of deaths, I found that 1 was due to dysentery, 7 to fever, and 10 to other causes, principally lung affections. Two possibly were famine cases, the deceased being mendicant musicians on their way from Nagpur to Chhindwara, who had died of fever. Otherwise mortality appeared to have been most prevalent among the Bhoyers, a thrifty set of cultivators, who in this village are all well-to-do. Two of the deceased were farm servants in regular employ, one a relative of the village carpenter, a well-to-do man, while a woman who gave birth to twins, both of whom died, helped to swell the total. The inhabitants assured me that none of the deceased had been in any straits with regard to food."

When it is remembered that the above death-rates occurred in the two tracts of this district were blessed above the others with a bumper harvest in the past year, I do not think that it is wrong to conclude that the present abnormal death-rate is due to causes with which privation has little to do directly. The active causes would appear to be malarial fever of a peculiarly fatal type, and dysentery induced by eating new grain.

LIST OF APPENDED STATEMENTS.

No. I.—Statement showing the Districts affected by the famine and the areas and populations returned a distressed on 31st May 1897.

Province and Division.	District.	Area of district.	Population of district.	Area returned as distressed.	Population of distressed area.
		Sq. m.		Sq. m.	
MADRAS.					
CIRCARS	Ganjam	8,360	1,897,000	2,678	908,000
	Vizagapatam ..	17,242	2,803,000	928	455,000
	Godavari ..	7,858	2,079,000	911	42,000
	Total ..	33,469	6,779,000	(a) 4,517	1,405,000
DECCAN	Kurnool	7,514	918,000	2,700	340,000
	Bellary	5,975	900,000	3,963	518,000
	Anantapur ..	4,886	709,000	4,517	584,000
	Cuddapah ..	8,731	1,272,000	2,244	391,000
	Total ..	27,106	3,799,000	13,424	1,833,000
	GRAND TOTAL..	60,575	10,578,000	(b) 17,941	3,238,000
BOMBAY.					
CENTRAL DIVISION..	Poona	5,349	1,068,000	2,987	488,000
	Satara	4,825	1,225,000	4,095	1,162,000
	Khandesh ..	10,700	1,430,000	(c) 10,700	1,430,000
	Sholapur	4,542	750,000	4,542	750,000
	Ahmednagar ..	6,645	888,000	6,645	888,000
	Nasik	5,817	843,000	5,817	843,000
	Total ..	37,878	6,204,000	34,786	5,561,000
SOUTHERN DIVISION	Bijapur	5,627	796,000	5,627	796,000
	Belgaum	4,674	1,013,000	1,642	353,000
	Total ..	10,301	1,809,000	7,269	1,149,000
	GRAND TOTAL..	48,179	8,013,000	42,055	6,710,000
BENGAL.					
PATNA	Shahabad ..	4,373	2,063,000	1,632	382,000
	Saran	2,656	2,467,000	1,512	1,416,000
	Champaran ..	3,531	1,860,000	3,531	1,860,000
	Muzaffarpur ..	3,004	2,711,000	1,851	1,660,000
	Darbhanga ..	3,335	2,801,000	2,940	2,234,000
	Total ..	16,899	11,902,000	11,466	7,552,000
CHOTA NAGPUR ..	Palamau	4,912	596,000	4,912	596,000
	Manbhum ..	4,147	1,193,000	3,373	991,000
	Total ..	9,059	1,789,000	8,285	1,587,000
PRESIDENCY	Nadia	2,793	1,644,000	927	478,000
	Khulna	2,077	1,177,000	467	276,000
	Murshidabad ..	2,144	1,250,000	167	95,000
	Total ..	7,014	4,071,000	1,561	849,000
BHAGALPUR	Bhagalpur ..	4,226	2,032,000	600	325,000
	Sonthal Parganas	5,470	1,754,000	1,321	377,000
	Total ..	9,696	3,786,000	1,921	702,000
ORISSA	Puri	2,473	945,000	365	102,000
	Total ..	2,473	945,000	365	102,000
	GRAND TOTAL..	45,141	22,493 000	23,598	10,792,000

Province and Division.	District.	Area of district.	Population of district.	Area returned as distressed.	Population of distressed area.
		Sq. m.		Sq. m.	
NORTH-WESTERN PROVINCES AND OUDH.					
AGRA	Agra	1,856	1,003,000	744	285,0[illegible]
	Etawah	1,694	727,000	271	62,00[illegible]
	Total ..	3,550	1,730,000	1,015	347,00[illegible]
ALLAHABAD	Cawnpore ..	2,363	1,210,000	1,219	462,00[illegible]
	Fatehpur.. ..	1,633	699,000	582	226,00[illegible]
	Banda	3,061	705,000	3,061	705,00[illegible]
	Hamirpur ..	2,289	513,000	2,289	513,0[illegible]
—	Allahabad ..	2,852	1,549,000	2,428	1,272,00[illegible]
	Jhansi	3,587	683,000	3,587	683,00[illegible]
	Jalaun	1,477	396,000	1,477	396,0[illegible]
	Total ..	17,262	5,755,000	14,643	4,257,00[illegible]
BENARES	Mirzapur.. ..	5,223	1,161,000	4,307	714,00[illegible]
	Jaunpur	1,550	1,265,000	271	214,00[illegible]
	Total ..	6,773	2,426,000	4,578	928,00[illegible]
GORAKHPUR ..	Gorakhpur ..	4,580	2,994,000	2,830	1,727,00[illegible]
	Azamgarh ..	2,148	1,729,000	1,130	914,00[illegible]
	Total ..	6,728	4,723,000	3,760	2,641,00[illegible]
LUCKNOW	Lucknow ..	967	774,000	967	77[illegible]
	Unao	1,736	953,000	1,736	953,0[illegible]
	Rae Bareli ..	1,752	1,037,000	1,752	1,037,0[illegible]
	Sitapur	2,255	1,075,000	1,520	703,0[illegible]
	Hardoi	2,325	1,113,000	2,325	1,113,0[illegible]
	Total ..	9,035	4,952,000	8,300	4,5[illegible]
	GRAND TOTAL..	43,348	19,586,000	(d) 32,296	12,7[illegible]
PUNJAB.					
DELHI	Hissar	5,217	776,000	3,763	544,[illegible]
	Rohtak	1,797	590,000	1,467	452,[illegible]
	Gurgaon	1,984	669,000	558	198,[illegible]
	Delhi	1,290	638,000	616	381,[illegible]
	Karnal	2,660	683,000	2,123	499,[illegible]
	Umballa	2,540	1,033,000	1,755	718,[illegible]
	Total ..	15,488	4,389,000	10,282	2,792,[illegible]
JULLUNDUR	Ferozepore ..	4,302	886,000	3,375	732,[illegible]
	Total ..	4,302	886,000	3,375	732,[illegible]
RAWALPINDI ..	Gujrat	2,051	760,000	562	155,[illegible]
	Total ..	2,051	760,000	562	155,[illegible]
	GRAND TOTAL..	21,841	6,035,000	14,219	3,679,[illegible]

No. I.—*Statement showing the Districts affected by the famine and the areas and population returned as distressed on 31st May 1897*—continued.

Province and Division.	District.	Area of district.	Population of district.	Area returned as distressed.	Population of distressed area.
		Sq. m.		Sq. m.	
CENTRAL PROVINCES.					
JUBBULPUR	Jubbulpur ..	3,946	748,000	3,853	498,000
	Saugor . ..	4,007	592,000	4,007	592,000
	Damoh	2,831	325,000	2,000	200,000
	Mandla	5,056	339,000	5,056	339,000
	Seoni	3,196	371,000	1,766	200,000
	Total ..	19,040	2,375,000	15,682	1,829,000
NAGPUR	Nagpur	3,832	758,000	524	243,000
	Bhandara ..	3,968	742,000	2,350	430,000
	Balaghat	3,164	383,000	1,500	230,000
	Chanda	10,749	697 000	2,052	104,000
	Wardha	2,428	400,000	650	70,000
	Total ..	24,141	2,980.000	7,076	1,077,000
NERBUDDA	Hoshangabad ..	4,024	499,000	3,794	361,000
	Narsingpur ..	1,916	367,000	1,916	367,000
	Nimar	3,928	285,000	3,928	285,000
	Chindwara ..	4,630	407,000	2,549	164,000
	Betul	3,824	323,000	2,868	149,000
	Total ..	18,892	1,912,000	15,055	1,326,000
CHHATTISGARH ..	Raipur	11,724	1,584,000	4,027	710,000
	Bilaspur	8,341	1,164,000	8,341	1,164,000
	Sambalpur ..	4,948	796,000	228	62,000
	Total ..	25,013	3,544,000	12,596	1,936,000
	GRAND TOTAL..	87,686	10,811,000	50,409	6,168,000
UPPER BURMA ..	Meiktila	2,178	217,000	2,178	217,000
	Yamethin ..	5,497	207,000	909	51,000
	Myingyan ..	2,774	352,000	1,873	260,000
	Total ..	10,449	776,000	4,960	528,000
BERARS	Akola	2,659	575,000	2,659	575,000
	Amraoti	2,759	655,000	2,759	655,000
	Basim	2,956	398,000	2,956	398,000
	Buldana	2,809	481,000	2,809	481,000
	Ellichpur ..	2,617	316,000	1,642	47,000
	Wun	3,911	471,000	3,911	471,000
	Total ..	17,711	2,896,000	16,737	2,627,000
	GRAND TOTAL, BRITISH INDIA	334,330	81,188,000	202,215	46,495,000
RAJPUTANA ..	Bhartpur ..	1,982	640,000	1,335	440,000
	Bikanir	22,340	832,000	18,750	587,000
	Dholpur	1,154	280,000	1,200	291,000
	Jaisalmir ..	16,062	115,000	16,000	115,000
	Marwar	34,963	2,520,000	6,000	235,000
	Tonk	1,113	199,000	595	114,000
	Total ..	77,516	4,586,000	44,070	1,782,000
CENTRAL INDIA..	Gwalior	10,227	1,508,000	4,200	771,000
	Baghelkand ..	25,846	3,482,000	12,000	1,778,000
	Bundelkand ..	11,323	1,738,000	9,940	1,428,000
	Total ..	47,396	6,728,000	26,140	3,977,000
HYDERABAD ..	Gulburgah ..	4,064	649,000	8,500 (Gulburgah, Raichur, Birh, Naldrug, Lingsagar)	1,102,000 (Gulburgah, Raichur, Birh, Naldrug, Lingsagar)
	Raichur	3,661	512,000		
	Birh	4,460	643,000		
	Naldrug	4,010	649,000		
	Lingsagar ..	4,907	620,000		
	Total ..	21,102	3,073,000	8,500	1,102,000
	GRAND TOTAL, NATIVE STATES	146,014	14,387,000	78,710	6,861,000
	GRAND TOTAL, BRITISH INDIA AND NATIVE STATES.. ..	480,344	95,575,000	280,925	53,356,000

(*a*) Distress was less general in this area than in the affected area in the Deccan.
(*b*) In August the affected area in the Madras Presidency was returned at 26,073 square miles with a population of 5,674,000, owing to spread of distress in the Circars.
(*c*) Of this area only 1,700 square miles with population of 250,000 were specially distressed. In the rest of Khandesh distress was slight and sporadic.
(*d*) Besides the area shown here as distressed in the North-Western Provinces and Oudh, 18 other districts were affected so as to require some relief measures.

N.B.—The figures in this table do not quite agree with the similar figures given on page 4 of the narrative. The reason is that this table shows the distressed areas and population as returned at one point of time (the 31st May 1897), whereas the figures on page 4 give what on the whole appears to be the fairest representation of the distressed areas and populations. The figures, it will be understood, varied from month to month.

No. II.—Statement of number of persons in rece[…]

Number.	Name of Province and District.	31st October 1896.	28th November 1896. Relief workers.	Dependants.	Gratuitous relief.	Total.	2nd January 1897. Relief workers.	Dependants.	Gratuitous relief.	Total.	30th January 1897. Relief workers.	Dependants.	Gratuitous relief.	Total.	27th February 1897. Relief workers.	Dependants.	Gratuitous relief.	Total.	3rd […] Relief workers.	Dependants.
	Madras.																			
1	Cuddapah ..	..	3,192	..	160	3,352	2,209	..	4,674	7,083	2,325	..	6,638	8,963	2,559	176	7,488	10,223	9,700	488
2	Kurnool ..	..	7,059	..	211	7,270	3,538	..	88	3,626	3,620	..	263	3,883	9,904	580	..	10,484	21,637	4,461
3	Bellary ..	..	15,249	..	1,451	16,700	13,462	..	1,799	15,261	22,860	..	2,853	25,713	31,515	2,272	751	37,538	46,540	2,639
4	Anantapur ..	..	1,008	..	80	1,088	334	..	26	360	3,306	..	373	3,679	4,294	411	..	4,705	7,334	412
5	Ganjam ..	..	..	..	..	..	..	..	..	..	..	..	125	125	1,494	..	1,391	2,885	185	..
6	Vizagapatam	..	..	..	..	..	..	..	..	..	..	..	..	..	..	..	..	..	3,868	..
7	Godavari ..	..	..	..	..	..	..	..	..	..	..	..	..	..	..	..	..	..	..	..
8	Kistna ..	..	..	..	..	..	..	..	..	..	..	..	..	..	..	..	..	..	..	..
	TOTAL ..	..	26,508	..	1,902	28,410	19,543	..	6,787	26,330	32,111	..	10,252	42,363	52,766	3,439	9,630	65,835	89,254	5,000
	Bombay.																			
1	Bijapur ..	..	..	..	..	..	44,542	14,099	2,274	60,915	58,282	18,225	4,932	81,439	55,673	19,907	8,162	83,742	51,652	16,079
2	Sholapur ..	..	..	..	..	..	40,257	19,133	1,721	61,111	55,865	27,617	3,729	87,211	70,141	34,906	6,385	111,432	86,630	40,049
3	Ahmednagar	..	2,382	..	..	2,382	27,546	11,008	4	38,558	31,870	16,383	27	48,280	58,603	30,408	1,829	90,840	65,077	30,763
4	Poona ..	..	..	..	..	..	13,064	6,865	2,811	22,740	17,074	7,958	2,273	27,305	15,514	5,084	3,644	24,242	14,225	2,749
5	Nasik ..	..	5,177	..	..	5,177	14,553	7,318	2	21,873	19,290	11,808	57	31,155	22,861	11,686	115	34,662	23,809	11,081
6	Satara ..	..	1,677	..	..	1,677	19,042	2,574	1	21,617	18,206	5,154	6	23,366	25,196	4,442	14	29,652	31,568	4,608
7	Khandesh ..	..	..	..	..	..	6,827	2,933	..	9,760	16,417	6,047	..	22,464	23,130	10,125	..	33,255	31,465	13,473
8	Belgaum ..	..	..	..	..	..	1,999	680	103	2,782	1,915	575	253	2,743	3,051	884	477	4,412	5,848	1,455
9	Dharwar ..	..	1,173	..	..	1,173	..	..	..	..	1,732	..	..	1,732	..	..	22	22	453	..
10	Ratnagiri ..	..	..	..	..	..	..	..	..	..	..	..	..	..	..	..	..	..	..	..
11	Kolaba ..	..	..	..	..	..	..	..	..	..	..	..	..	..	..	..	..	..	..	..
	TOTAL ..	..	10,409	..	..	10,409	167,830	64,610	6,916	239,356	220,651	93,767	11,277	325,695	274,169	117,442	20,648	412,259	310,727	[illegible]
	Bengal.																			
1	Champaran ..	..	1,937	..	..	1,937	48,684	..	2,424	51,108	97,149	..	5,808	102,957	130,804	..	39,447	170,251	89,360	[illegible]
2	Shahabad ..	..	1,002	..	..	1,002	1,145	..	..	1,145	2,274	..	..	2,274	1,225	..	4,740	5,965	10,668	[illegible]
3	Nadia ..	..	445	..	..	445	2,385	..	..	2,385	6,060	..	770	6,830	10,578	..	..	10,578	13,220	[illegible]
4	Patna ..	..	..	..	..	..	311	..	..	311	587	..	36	623	..	..	61	61	..	..
5	Khulna ..	..	..	..	..	..	111	..	..	111	147	..	21	168	1,861	..	..	1,861	2,308	..
6	Saran ..	..	..	..	..	..	3,655	..	1,770	5,425	13,811	..	12,070	25,881	14,792	..	17,304	32,096	14,202	..
7	Darbhanga ..	..	..	..	..	..	28,567	..	..	28,567	135,644	..	55,283	190,927	80,015	2,566	57,512	140,093	109,570	10,663
8	Muzaffarpur	..	..	..	..	..	2,358	..	..	2,358	6,911	..	1,703	8,614	16,656	120	11,099	27,875	34,445	2,025
9	Rajshahi ..	..	..	..	..	..	..	..	..	..	536	..	..	536	585	..	..	585	591	..
10	Bhagalpur ..	..	..	..	..	..	..	..	..	..	..	..	..	..	7,790	370	..	8,160	8,597	54
11	Palamau ..	..	..	..	..	..	..	..	..	..	..	..	..	..	3,949	..	253	4,202	4,020	..
12	Manbhum ..	..	..	..	..	..	..	..	..	..	..	..	..	..	3,492	..	4,000	7,492	3,901	..
13	Pubna ..	..	..	..	..	..	..	..	..	..	..	..	..	..	53	..	..	53	323	..
14	Murshidabad	..	..	..	..	..	..	..	..	..	..	..	..	..	730	..	..	730	3,983	..
15	Hazaribagh ..	..	..	..	..	..	..	..	..	..	..	..	..	..	..	..	..	..	2,062	..
16	Puri ..	..	..	..	..	..	..	..	..	..	..	..	..	..	..	..	..	..	4,035	31
17	Sontal Parganas.	..	..	..	..	..	..	..	..	..	..	..	..	..	..	..	..	..	2,162	18
18	Bankura ..	..	..	..	..	..	..	..	..	..	..	..	..	..	..	..	..	..	..	..
19	Singhbhum ..	..	..	..	..	..	..	..	..	..	..	..	..	..	..	..	..	..	..	..
20	Lohardaga ..	..	..	..	..	..	..	..	..	..	..	..	..	..	..	..	..	..	..	..
21	Jessore ..	..	..	..	..	..	..	..	..	..	..	..	..	..	..	..	..	..	..	..
22	Dinajpur ..	..	..	..	..	..	..	..	..	..	..	..	..	..	..	..	..	..	..	..
	TOTAL ..	..	3,384	..	..	3,384	87,216	..	4,194	91,410	263,119	..	75,691	338,810	272,530	3,056	134,416	410,002	303,447	[illegible]

relief at the end of each month.

1st May 1897.				29th May 1897.				3rd July 1897.				31st July 1897.				28th August 1897.			
Relief workers.	Dependants.	Gratuitous relief.	Total.	Relief workers.	Dependants.	Gratuitous relief.	Total.	Relief workers.	Dependants.	Gratuitous relief.	Total.	Relief workers.	Dependants.	Gratuitous relief.	Total.	Relief workers.	Dependants.	Gratuitous relief.	Total.
32,228	1,211	9,856	43,295	47,371	1,575	16,152	65,098	82,070	2,597	25,628	110,295	99,336	2,993	22,385	124,714	44,730	1,971	26,696	73,397
56,967	2,838	3,765	63,570	87,525	4,568	11,190	103,283	120,430	4,528	40,190	165,148	152,566	5,360	61,099	219,025	126,543	5,498	49,658	181,699
66,622	4,653	3,886	75,161	94,348	4,811	10,731	109,890	114,571	6,259	20,766	141,596	155,270	6,403	27,308	188,981	149,741	6,580	28,966	185,287
18,278	893	988	20,159	42,417	1,823	7,577	51,817	56,512	2,888	9,808	69,208	63,375	3,703	10,822	77,900	61,500	3,589	10,986	76,075
5,637	..	10,625	16,262	17,523	..	31,253	48,776	36,062	67	54,867	90,996	47,059	224	96,533	143,816	9,305	65	32,744	42,114
11,767	671	855	13,293	14,754	970	1,325	17,049	23,351	1,885	17,626	42,862	19,416	1,211	31,031	51,658	12,362	543	14,892	27,797
..	..	..	..	500	..	..	500	..	..	..	..	155	..	728	883	150	..	6,001	6,151
..	..	..	..	..	..	..	..	..	..	..	..	..	..	..	..	640	..	..	640
191,409	10,266	29,975	231,650	304,438	13,747	78,228	396,413	432,996	18,224	168,885	620,105	537,177	19,894	249,906	806,977	404,971	18,246	169,943	593,160
53,634	15,913	9,687	79,234	45,866	6,975	10,974	63,815	57,753	9,644	13,787	81,184	92,136	12,323	13,397	117,856	118,806	18,428	15,564	152,798
92,068	31,600	8,271	131,939	83,008	25,371	8,152	116,531	70,852	22,308	8,935	102,095	80,846	26,470	11,118	118,434	81,293	24,680	13,432	119,405
55,436	11,676	5,175	72,287	44,379	11,757	6,194	62,330	39,444	12,673	9,417	61,534	59,809	16,524	15,017	91,350	49,421	15,243	20,349	85,013
19,963	2,759	5,787	28,509	22,350	3,269	7,802	33,421	9,181	2,178	10,472	21,831	10,917	2,571	11,549	25,037	13,387	3,239	14,849	31,475
19,774	6,444	199	26,417	17,901	7,587	629	26,117	10,498	4,727	1,635	16,860	6,836	2,780	1,588	11,204	3,661	1,425	1,409	6,495
20,639	2,595	87	23,321	9,478	1,818	195	11,491	9,217	1,526	658	11,401	10,643	1,423	2,158	14,224	7,028	459	4,519	12,006
22,287	5,987	..	28,274	17,641	5,536	..	23,177	8,216	2,614	..	10,830	8,984	2,734	..	11,718	2,012	897	525	3,434
9,606	2,433	517	12,556	9,824	2,579	580	12,983	7,968	1,236	820	10,024	13,299	1,967	770	16,036	17,036	2,531	921	20,488
273	..	893	1,166	612	..	997	1,609	365	..	1,119	1,484	2,115	..	1,006	3,121	3,441	..	1,066	4,507
115	..	..	115	262	..	..	262	..	..	..	..	..	..	..	..	155	..	..	155
..	..	..	..	298	..	..	298	..	..	..	..	..	..	..	..	..	..	..	..
293,725	79,477	30,616	403,818	251,619	64,892	35,523	352,034	213,494	56,906	46,843	317,243	285,585	66,702	56,603	408,980	296,240	66,902	72,634	435,776
72,027	6,041	61,011	139,079	104,727	8,433	79,815	192,975	52,708	3,642	85,321	141,671	14,808	961	53,519	69,288	12,489	133	28,340	40,962
7,563	1,358	21,937	30,858	9,322	2,252	21,914	33,488	1,797	361	19,161	21,319	..	..	23,861	23,861	..	..	17,518	17,518
19,661	9,385	20,085	49,131	20,471	10,696	60,160	91,327	24,502	..	68,426	92,928	14,337	..	50,362	64,699	331	..	7,339	7,670
..	..	121	121	..	..	..	..	..	..	188	188	..	..	237	237	..	..	1,588	1,588
3,764	..	5,360	9,124	4,809	..	6,379	11,188	1,018	..	10,434	11,452	285	..	7,365	7,650	..	..	6,086	6,086
24,674	102	48,873	73,649	24,177	1,890	57,026	83,093	13,252	1,293	47,705	62,250	18,152	1,618	57,963	77,733	11,178	284	40,349	51,811
131,363	9,302	66,597	207,262	147,423	9,714	78,662	35,799	107,720	7,336	96,759	211,815	57,520	3,966	95,895	157,381	14,206	321	76,797	91,324
54,245	4,566	55,141	113,952	58,841	3,748	59,201	121,790	37,135	1,275	71,974	110,384	36,472	412	64,602	101,486	19,775	651	47,094	67,520
781	..	..	781	360	..	..	360	405	..	..	405	571	..	..	571	..	..	..	..
20,959	1,087	2,815	24,861	7,287	..	2,750	10,037	718	..	9,098	9,816	..	..	6,216	6,216	..	..	..	..
2,839	..	1,989	4,828	3,023	..	2,145	5,168	1,726	..	2,002	3,728	1,586	..	2,399	3,985	1,064	..	2,369	3,433
3,899	..	5,932	9,831	3,977	..	11,987	15,964	7,524	..	6,781	14,305	9,123	..	7,436	16,559	15,501	..	8,904	24,405
492	..	..	492	679	..	15	694	1,522	..	1,883	3,405	447	..	52	499	37	..	16	53
3,517	..	..	3,517	3,808	..	4,732	8,540	2,281	..	4,604	6,885	5,013	..	..	5,013	406	..	..	406
3,408	..	2,160	5,568	2,797	..	4,547	7,344	2,586	..	3,945	6,531	951	454	3,220	4,625	514	..	1,401	1,915
3,178	47	182	3,407	3,618	194	224	4,036	3,727	..	1,482	5,209	2,974	..	1,265	4,239	2,052	..	1,197	3,249
2,180	110	221	2,511	1,680	49	902	2,631	2,413	..	3,989	6,402	1,305	17	4,350	5,672	..	..	..	..
..	..	..	..	5,347	..	3,521	8,868	1,355	..	8,986	10,341	1,167	253	8,489	9,909	3,534	..	10,195	13,529
..	..	..	..	..	..	..	..	82	..	..	82	..	..	..	..	..	..	..	..
..	..	..	..	..	..	..	..	..	..	..	..	585	..	1,255	1,840	1,008	..	3,207	4,215
..	..	..	..	..	..	..	..	..	..	..	..	309	..	..	309	38	..	..	38
..	..	..	..	..	..	..	..	..	..	..	..	117	..	..	117	54	..	..	54
[illegible]4,550	31,998	292,424	678,972	402,346	36,976	394,125	833,447	262,471	13,916	442,729	719,116	166,429	6,974	388,486	561,889	81,987	1,389	252,400	335,776

No. II.—Statement of number of persons in re

Number.	Name of Province and District.	31st October 1896.	28th November 1896. Relief workers.	Dependants.	Gratuitous relief.	Total.	2nd January 1897. Relief workers.	Dependants.	Gratuitous relief.	Total.	30th January 1897. Relief workers.	Dependants.	Gratuitous relief.	Total.	27th February 1897. Relief workers.	Dependants.	Gratuitous relief.	Total.	Relief workers.	D[illegible]
	North-Western Provinces and Oudh.																			
1	Agra ..	..	2,163	..	91	2,254	4,897	..	247	5,144	17,525	3,956	823	22,304	18,541	7,080	6,783	32,354	7,789	..
2	Etawah ..	..	..	..	..	..	4,846	..	779	5,625	10,114	2,493	2,394	15,001	13,701	3,678	2,960	20,339	750	..
3	Banda ..	4,586	31,166	9,773	7,3 65	48,304	67,140	18,192	12,780	98,112	109,775	25,707	17,381	152,863	142,296	29,303	28,439	201,038	131,816	23,72
4	Cawnpore ..	..	..	..	1,063	1,063	11,945	2,910	3,607	18,462	40,712	9,206	18,949	68,867	81.739	17,739	19,847	119,325	4,757	1,114
5	Hamirpur ..	8,593	3,565	1,890	4,716	10,171	15,056	3,592	6,240	24,888	38,400	11,219	10,382	60,001	36,532	8,323	15,627	60,482	62,401	13,03
6	Allahabad ..	..	10,095	455	3,728	14,278	59,184	23,601	12,129	94,914	136,040	26,888	20,423	183,351	119,729	32,031	29,034	180,794	114,928	22,2[illegible]
7	Jhansi ..	1,735	7,064	1,624	1,217	9,905	11,329	2,075	3,116	16,520	34,436	6,551	6,019	47,006	47.484	10,455	9,447	67,386	48,667	9,87[illegible]
8	Jalaun ..	7,718	10,281	983	2,497	13,761	17,704	4,663	4,384	26,731	48,555	10,623	21,516	80,694	72,180	19,682	10,259	102,121	54,212	15,06[illegible]
9	Jaunpur ..	5,185	6,923	2,068	149	9,140	14,825	3,919	589	19,333	31,158	10,011	1,882	43,051	44,745	15,158	11,370	71,273	8,966	1,033
10	Gorakhpur ..	..	..	..	714	714	2,024	..	3,117	5,141	13,181	1,764	7,193	22,138	32,872	5,606	6,164	44,642	26,572	3,656
11	Lucknow ..	460	372	..	1,116	1,488	14,251	1,658	10,521	26,430	34,215	7,298	14,795	56.308	69,421	17,013	21,047	107,481	20,806	1,529
12	Unao ..	..	..	..	..	..	8,028	961	1,378	10,367	28,604	6.169	5,667	40.440	37,114	11,803	11,174	6,091	5,670	..
13	Rae Bareli ..	7,012	11,661	2,303	1,388	15,352	21,351	6,930	1,568	29,849	55,935	14,587	8,622	79,144	61,696	17,057	12,105	90,858	14,765	7[illegible]
14	Sitapur ..	..	4,086	121	250	4,457	18,190	2,617	507	21,314	31,883	5,508	6,717	44,103	38,830	7,698	21,170	67,707	..	..
15	Hardoi ..	5,591	7,460	1,781	1,938	11,179	20,425	6,527	11,972	38,924	65,483	17,618	93,474	176,575	93,552	25,315	25,947	144,814	42,940	10,67[illegible]
16	Bara Banki ..	..	2,657	..	119	2,776	10,763	..	811	11,574	21,081	2,928	3,069	27,078	14,859	2,277	4,463	21,599	505	..
17	Mirzapur ..	..	..	..	..	..	1,400	..	795	2,195	12,201	3,000	2,781	18,072	44,627	11,542	9,441	65,610	30,161	8,774
18	Azamgarh ..	..	369	..	..	369	9,627	..	1,083	10,710	3,906	..	5,241	9,147	7,291	1,268	7,795	16,354	2,668	..
19	Fatehpur ..	..	..	..	..	..	199	..	938	1,137	3,853	..	7,000	10,853	18,718	5,044	10,006	33,768	4,994	611
20	Dehra Dun ..	..	..	..	..	..	..	..	..	..	350	..	..	350	360	..	..	360	475	..
21	Bijnor ..	..	..	..	..	..	251	..	453	704	2,419	..	768	3,187	2,728	..	1,423	4,151	..	..
22	Moradabad ..	..	..	..	..	..	107	..	134	241	2,426	..	410	2,830	5,481	..	1,557	7,038	62	..
23	Bareilly ..	..	..	..	..	..	518	..	106	624	5,238	..	230	5,468	3,565	..	2,115	5,680	..	..
24	Muttra ..	..	..	..	..	..	3,399	..	156	3,555	8,429	..	1,032	9,461	22,451	..	4,562	27,013	240	..
25	Etah	..	..	..	..	..	1,000	..	596	1,596	707	..	1,783	2,490	960	..	1,834	2,794	..	..
26	Mainpuri ..	..	..	..	..	..	77	..	167	244	37	..	700	737	132	..	585	717	..	..
27	Farukhabad	..	..	..	..	..	1,174	..	807	1,981	1,867	..	2,242	4,109	546	..	10,904	11,450	..	..
28	Budaun ..	..	..	..	..	..	668	..	106	774	2,071	..	142	2,213	960	..	294	1,254	..	..
29	Shahjahanpur	..	..	..	..	..	753	..	1,556	2,309	2,436	..	1,885	4,321	3,317	..	2,694	6,011	62	..
30	Pilibhit ..	..	..	..	..	..	..	..	396	396	8,481	..	418	8,899	6,563	..	1,220	7,783	296	..
31	Kheri ..	..	..	..	..	..	230	..	19	249	2,614	..	190	2,804	830	..	473	1,303	130	..
32	Sultanpur ..	..	..	..	..	..	2,661	..	1,238	3,899	9,774	..	2,294	12,068	12,748	..	3,300	15,948	342	..
33	Partabgarh ..	..	..	..	..	..	3,632	..	428	4,060	2,233	..	6,360	8,593	15,253	..	5,657	20,910	177	..
34	Fyzabad ..	..	..	..	..	..	1,943	..	1,180	3,123	8,942	..	4,284	13,226	7,274	..	4,521	11,795	280	..
35	Benares ..	..	..	..	..	..	318	..	604	922	666	..	950	1,616	243	..	561	804	..	..
36	Gonda ..	..	..	..	..	..	2,163	..	1,480	3,648	7,289	..	2,272	9,561	4,801	..	3,203	8,004	389	..
37	Basti	..	155	..	331	486	515	..	670	1,185	2,657	..	2,522	5,179	4,708	..	1,770	6,478	1,467	[illegible]
	Total ..	40,890	98,017	20,998	26,882	145,697	332,593	77,645	86,637	496,875	805,695	165,611	282,802	1,254,108	1,089,856	248,022	300,651	[illegible]	587,312	111,67[illegible]

relief at the end of each month—continued.

	1st May 1897.				29th May 1897.				3rd July 1897.				31st July 1897.				28th August 1897.			
	Relief workers.	Dependants.	Gratuitous relief.	Total.	Relief workers.	Dependants.	Gratuitous relief.	Total.	Relief workers.	Dependants.	Gratuitous relief.	Total.	Relief workers.	Dependants.	Gratuitous relief.	Total.	Relief workers.	Dependants.	Gratuitous relief.	Total.
117	15,990	47	7,492	23,520	20,114	135	6,348	26,597	23,913	..	8,110	32,023	7,983	..	7,208	15,191	3,386	..	6,916	10,302
239	1,776	..	2,893	4,669	1,698	..	3,536	5,234	972	..	3,511	4,483	30	..	3,100	3,130	..	..	878	878
127	159,789	25,835	35,129	220,753	226,516	30,796	40,164	297,476	139,056	22,091	54,251	215,398	29,190	5,408	75,930	110,528	6,046	1,520	73,226	80,792
146	1,370	15	8,696	10,081	2,251	413	9,659	12,323	503	..	8,947	9,450	..	..	10,456	10,456	..	..	4,073	4,073
355	78,853	14,925	22,235	114,013	89,857	15,338	22,362	127,557	6,088	1,849	21,636	29,573	762	224	21,110	22,096	..	..	14,500	14,500
587	189,462	39,371	45,884	274,717	227,865	51,050	50,809	329,724	29,942	8,217	60,436	98,495	13,755	4,372	59,764	77,891	5,614	1,728	37,133	44,475
340	45,142	9,381	17,980	72,503	65,158	12,913	19,350	97,421	6,367	877	22,140	29,384	1,272	366	22,541	24,179	596	166	19,716	20,478
388	84,925	25,048	28,121	138,094	83,847	21,595	18,246	123,688	6,720	2,013	21,150	29,883	2,881	905	31,027	31,813	..	..	19,808	19,808
370	13,899	..	16,169	30,048	20,432	2,534	20,296	43,262	2,649	..	16,769	19,418	..	..	22,216	22,216	..	..	23,392	23,392
572	16,491	..	11,514	28,005	15,055	..	12,408	27,463	11,597	..	17,462	29,059	3,943	..	12,436	16,379	..	..	9,545	9,545
293	24,215	1,012	24 215	40,442	27,135	5,490	23,876	56,510	27,210	5,265	25,280	57,755	16,075	3,926	25,193	45,194	907	215	15,158	16,280
732	8,844	554	15,545	24,943	19,016	4,208	16,065	39,289	9,342	3,033	16,556	28,931	303	124	19,559	19,986	..	..	17,812	17,813
545	15,317	726	12,230	28,273	17,959	3,829	13,419	35,307	9,837	2,674	15,806	28,317	1,375	488	16,662	18,525	687	367	13,303	14,357
667	366	..	3,995	4,361	572	129	3,627	4,328	242	..	5,502	5,744	..	..	4,425	4,425	..	..	3,374	3,374
548	83,423	21,241	32,423	137,086	88,178	22,074	40,598	150,850	53,460	13,960	46,072	113,492	2,768	802	48,133	51,703	1,772	493	43,357	45,622
537	866	..	726	1,594	1,022	..	1,033	2,055	..	..	1,299	,299	..	..	1,441	1,441	..	..	1,459	1,459
257	31,844	6,047	17,580	55,471	29,675	8,240	20,157	58,072	5,700	1,697	20,626	28,023	1,991	615	12,616	15,222	674	119	11,327	12,120
911	7,002	..	3,387	10,389	12,320	186	5,569	18,075	3,114	..	17,257	20,371	553	..	15,033	15,586	..	..	10,409	10,409
177	5,135	1,386	7,928	14,449	6,531	1,545	8,710	16,786	2,127	660	8,690	11,477	382	176	9,280	9,838	..	..	8,190	8,190
475	..	..	..	..	..	..	..	..	..	..	..	..	..	..	..	..	..	..	..	..
284	..	..	718	718	108	..	862	970	846	..	1,282	2,128	..	..	1,608	1,608	..	..	1,391	1,391
767	..	..	2,657	2,657	664	..	2,574	3,238	2,362	..	2,894	5,256	..	..	3,597	3,597	..	..	1,221	1,221
596	..	..	2,008	2,008	1,211	..	1,913	3,124	1,713	..	1,593	3,306	938	..	1,899	2,837	..	..	851	851
646	1,441	..	3,569	5,010	3,333	..	3,190	6,523	3,119	..	4,651	7,770	..	..	3,972	3,972	..	..	1,689	1,689
290	..	..	596	596	5	..	1,464	1,469	..	..	2,183	2,183	..	..	2,052	2,052	..	..	775	775
38	..	..	33	33	..	..	597	597	..	..	470	470	..	..	686	686	..	..	2,414	2,414
570	54	..	2,829	2,883	85	..	2,465	2,550	38	..	3,608	3,646	..	..	2,891	2,891	..	..	1,366	1,366
029	..	..	1,425	1,425	283	..	1,135	1,418	..	..	175	175	..	..	397	397	..	..	284	284
106	303	..	3,828	4,131	533	..	3,158	3,691	231	..	4,291	4,522	..	..	5,604	5,604	..	..	2,749	2,749
568	375	..	2,665	3,040	1,047	..	1,514	2,561	1,605	..	3,534	3,139	261	..	3,205	3,466	..	..	2,072	2,072
180	..	..	..	..	706	..	123	829	1,253	..	281	1,534	..	..	945	945	..	..	385	385
372	1,273	..	1,158	2,431	3,018	..	1,448	4,466	269	..	2,394	2,663	..	..	2,363	2,363	..	..	1,488	1,488
374	397	..	2,069	2,486	3,069	..	3,363	6,432	318	..	3,772	4,090	..	..	4,082	4,082	..	..	2,468	2,468
564	30	..	2,802	2,832	..	..	2,289	2,289	..	..	4,700	4,700	..	..	3,375	3,375	..	..	501	501
352	[illegible]	..	10,498	10,498	1,479	..	12,268	13,747	..	..	12,033	12,033	..	..	11,123	11,123	..	..	17,163	17,163
416	[illegible]	..	366	701	1,614	..	304	1,918	..	..	568	568	..	..	2,578	2,578	..	..	2,456	2,456
342	[illegible]	..	1,027	3,306	1,586	..	1,661	3,247	170	..	2,110	2,280	..	..	1,827	1,827	..	..	568	568
	[illegible]	146,886	352,309	1,287,195	973,942	180,484	376,580	1,530,986	350,663	62,336	442,039	855,038	84,462	17,406	470,334	572,202	19,682	4,608	373,417	397,707
	…et Indian Charitable Relief Fund		38,699	38,699	Deduct Relief Fund.		59,863	59,863	Deduct Charitable Relief Fund.		56,426	56,486	Deduct Relief Fund.		66,726	66,726				
		Balance	313,610	1,248,496		Balance	316,697	1,471,123		Balance	385,553	798,552		Balance	403,608	505,476				

No. II.—Statement of number of persons in r

Number.	Name of Province and District.	31st October 1896.	28th November 1896. Relief workers.	Dependants.	Gratuitous relief.	Total.	2nd January 1897. Relief workers.	Dependants.	Gratuitous relief.	Total.	30th January 1897. Relief workers.	Dependants.	Gratuitous relief.	Total.	27th February 1897. Relief workers.	Dependants.	Gratuitous relief.	Total.	3[illegible] Relief workers.	Dependants.
	Punjab.																			
1	Hissar ..	..	..	..	..	..	13,004	..	..	13,004	23,494	..	5,715	29,209	37,258	9,842	2,928	50,028	39,251	12,044
2	Rohtak ..	..	..	..	..	..	819	..	..	819	3,614	..	2,185	5,799	2,714	709	2,992	6,415	4,349	1,400
3	Gurgaon ..	..	..	..	..	..	..	..	..	..	1,552	..	37	1,589	2,402	..	81	2,483	1,070	33
4	Delhi ..	..	..	..	..	..	152	..	..	152	3,044	..	696	3,740	2,603	..	959	3,562	1,024	116
5	Karnal ..	570	..	..	..	..	2,950	..	..	2,950	2,351	..	114	2,465	1,991	161	4	2,156	5,840	3,321
6	Umballa ..	..	69	..	..	69	1,167	..	..	1,167	1,003	..	..	1,003	3,726	304	618	4,648	1,847	184
7	Ferozepur ..	..	..	..	..	..	2,833	..	..	2,833	2,080	..	228	2,308	2,005	240	..	2,245	1,496	..
8	Multan ..	..	..	..	..	..	107	..	..	107	302	..	..	302	126	9	..	135	102	..
9	Lahore ..	..	..	..	..	..	600	..	..	600	2,163	..	..	2,163	2,173	..	..	2,173	2,001	..
10	Sialkot ..	..	..	..	..	..	284	..	..	284	270	..	..	270	..	..	..	..	..	..
11	Gujrat ..	5,332	10,850	..	..	10,850	22,491	8,027	..	30,518	32,780	..	15,177	47,957	28,136	3,500	18,000	49,636	12,168	72[illegible]
12	Gujranwala	..	..	..	..	..	297	..	..	297	217	..	..	217	..	..	..	..	..	..
13	Rawalpindi	..	..	..	..	..	226	..	..	226	112	..	..	112	43	..	..	43	..	..
14	Ludhiana ..	..	..	..	..	..	116	..	..	116	125	..	..	125	137	..	77	214	79	..
	TOTAL ..	5,902	10,919	..	..	10,919	45,046	8,027	..	53,073	73,107	..	24,152	97,259	83,314	14,765	25,659	123,738	69,227	17,913
	Central Provinces.																			
1	Saugor ..	..	..	..	..	..	..	..	..	27,619	26,969	..	9,616	36,585	23,904	3,672	9,754	37,330	32,715	3,014
2	Damoh ..	..	..	..	..	..	..	..	..	12,372	18,923	..	1,905	20,828	14,571	2,022	1,447	18,040	21,248	3,114
3	Jubbulpore ..	..	..	..	..	..	..	..	..	36,077	70,178	..	13,727	83,905	70,103	6,262	10,020	86,385	65,142	9,139
4	Mandla ..	..	..	..	..	..	..	..	..	12,733	14,260	..	862	15,142	20,639	..	4,788	25,427	16,769	3,8[illegible]
5	Seoni	..	..	..	..	..	..	..	..	6,587	4,142	..	3,401	7,543	5,454	1,059	2,003	8,516	8,419	1,433
6	Narsinghpur	..	..	..	..	..	..	..	..	8,730	18,043	2,179	4,056	24,278	13,981	3,444	3,013	20,438	35,001	7,362
7	Hoshangabad	..	..	..	..	..	..	..	..	23,814	30,907	..	6,033	36,940	20,209	..	6,926	27,135	38,100	7,985
8	Nimar ..	..	..	..	..	..	..	..	..	853	558	125	67	750	192	79	114	385	229	20
9	Betul ..	..	..	..	..	..	..	..	..	2,935	10,747	872	688	12,307	14,100	1,636	864	16,600	7,398	642
10	Chindwara ..	..	..	..	..	..	..	..	..	3,388	4,950	..	1,843	6,793	5,989	1,419	1,393	8,801	7,159	1,468
11	Nagpur ..	..	..	..	..	..	..	..	..	4,208	1,312	..	830	2,142	1,278	270	958	2,506	5,062	1,012
12	Chanda ..	..	..	..	..	..	..	..	..	640	2,643	250	12	2,905	2,690	392	..	3,082	..	..
13	Bhandara ..	..	..	..	..	..	..	..	..	7,633	9,118	936	512	10,566	15,094	3,420	1,326	19,840	10,371	2,5[illegible]
14	Balaghat ..	..	..	..	..	..	..	..	..	8,0[illegible]0	5,219	..	1,662	6,881	10,348	3,000	1,466	14,814	25,244	6,222
15	Raipur ..	..	..	..	..	..	..	..	..	10,650	7,658	..	1,377	9,035	37,757	..	6,173	43,930	49,853	11,044
16	Bilaspur ..	..	..	..	..	..	..	..	..	700	6,244	108	1,340	7,687	12,012	1,765	4,257	18,034	20,955	1,5[illegible]
17	Sambalpur ..	..	..	..	..	..	..	..	..	..	..	..	..	..	..	..	..	..	..	..
18	Wardha ..	..	..	..	..	..	..	..	..	25	..	..	..	..	..	..	..	..	..	..
	TOTAL ..	..	..	..	..	..	..	..	..	167,189	231,871	4,465	47,951	284,287	268,321	28,440	54,502	351,263	345,[illegible]	[illegible]
	Burma.																			
1	Meiktila						14,691	..	2,447	17,138	17,277	..	3,135	20,412	13,642	..	2,290	15,932	6,830	..
2	Myingyan	2,998	20,337	..	..	20,337	10,036	..	2,643	12,679	9,689	..	2,806	12,495	8,075	..	1,785	9,860	12,829	..
3	Yamethin						..	..	317	317	..	..	323	323	..	..	336	336	..	..
	TOTAL ..	2,998	20,337	..	..	20,337	24,727	..	5,407	30,134	26,966	..	6,264	33,230	21,717	..	4,411	26,128	19,659	..
	Berar.																			
1	Akola ..	..	..	..	..	..	..	..	..	..	..	..	..	..					9,313	..
2	Basim ..	..	..	..	..	..	..	..	..	..	..	..	..	..	..	..	..	11,111	2,105	..
3	Ellichpur ..	..	..	..	..	..	..	..	..	..	..	..	..	..					2,507	..
4	Amraoti ..	..	..	..	..	..	..	..	..	..	..	..	..	..	..	..	..	..	..	..
5	Buldana ..	..	..	..	..	..	..	..	..	..	..	..	..	..	..	..	..	..	1,702	..
6	Wun	..	..	..	..	..	..	..	..	..	..	..	..	..	..	..	..	..	..	..
	TOTAL ..	..	..	..	..	..	..	..	..	..	..	..	..	..	..	..	..	11,111	15,697	..

relief at the end of each month—concluded.

	1st May 1897.				29th May 1897.				3rd July 1897.				31st July 1897.				28th August 1897.			
Total.	Relief workers.	Dependants.	Gratuitous relief.	Total.	Relief workers.	Dependants.	Gratuitous relief.	Total.	Relief workers.	Dependants.	Gratuitous relief.	Total.	Relief workers.	Dependants.	Gratuitous relief.	Total.	Relief workers.	Dependants.	Gratuitous relief.	Total.
7,521	45,548	10,792	7,892	64,232	47,448	10,457	9,342	67,247	63,447	5,611	7,783	76,841	19,266	2,792	7,757	29,815	6,838	1,515	7,010	15,363
4,347	5,054	1,343	2,141	8,538	6,678	1,540	2,193	10,411	6,730	1,493	2,135	10,358	45	..	2,118	2,163	..	..	61	61
1,644	443	18	56	517	..	..	..	..	..	..	..	..	..	..	..	..	..	..	..	..
1,864	958	87	536	1,581	767	206	839	1,812	1,070	458	945	2,473	..	..	691	691	..	..	651	651
10,774	3,039	1,285	1,548	5,872	3,886	2,273	1,358	7,517	3,676	1,150	1,370	6,196	1,300	..	882	2,182	1,116	..	209	1,325
2,397	464	722	203	1,389	2,131	..	1,780	3,911	460	..	634	1,094	..	..	550	550	..	..	147	147
1,306	73	..	..	73	360	..	..	300	535	..	..	535	509	..	..	509	..	..	..	..
102	..	..	..	..	..	..	..	..	..	..	..	..	..	..	..	..	..	..	..	..
2,001	91	..	..	91	..	..	..	..	..	..	..	..	..	..	..	..	..	..	..	..
..	..	..	..	..	..	..	..	..	..	..	..	..	..	..	..	..	..	..	..	..
16,129	5,041	..	539	5,580	3,807	789	469	5,065	..	..	..	..	..	..	..	..	..	..	..	..
..	..	..	..	..	..	..	..	..	..	..	..	..	..	..	..	..	..	..	..	..
..	66	..	..	66	45	..	..	45	143	..	..	143	..	..	..	..	..	..	..	..
99	23	..	9	32	..	..	..	..	..	..	..	..	..	..	..	..	..	..	..	..
2,471	60,800	14,247	12,924	87,971	65,122	15,265	15,981	90,368	70,061	8,712	12,867	97,640	21,120	2,792	11,998	35,910	7,954	1,515	8,078	17,547
7,956	31,456	3,361	13,534	48,351	38,162	4,379	15,773	58,313	18,776	1,886	14,882	35,544	23,251	2,485	12,057	37,793	11,584	257	16,308	28,149
41,026	30,432	4,652	8,656	43,742	36,060	5,864	12,099	54,023	32,651	5,348	13,108	51,107	32,060	5,809	13,939	52,408	10,756	2,027	15,562	28,315
8,752	64,362	8,772	39,042	112,176	53,152	8,341	22,167	83,660	24,667	2,770	22,494	49,931	34,004	4,065	38,934	77,003	19,407	3,712	45,070	68,189
24,570	23,021	5,234	2,388	30,643	24,243	5,607	3,119	32,969	11,838	1,810	3,746	17,394	11,107	2,251	4,453	17,811	12,388	3,107	16,527	32,022
10,521	11,717	2,428	884	15,029	12,372	1,768	2,601	16,741	6,597	793	3,168	10,558	4,974	1,047	5,270	11,291	2,986	1,212	12,999	17,197
45,350	18,847	2,768	2,534	24,149	42,154	6,643	3,355	52,152	14,390	2,131	5,835	22,356	19,720	3,108	9,349	32,177	19,790	2,725	14,400	36,915
48,946	44,079	8,349	868	53,296	55,988	9,304	856	66,148	23,273	4,788	3,909	31,970	34,521	6,602	5,600	46,783	29,563	5,490	7,787	42,840
400	133	37	309	479	342	32	512	886	64	11	838	913	688	105	1,040	1,833	811	228	1,401	2,470
5,890	8,937	1,685	1,530	12,152	15,341	2,920	1,880	20,141	7,299	509	2,258	10,066	9,290	671	3,149	13,110	8,499	..	4,983	13,484
16,552	10,807	1,603	1,910	14,320	12,866	1,961	2,054	16,881	12,040	1,541	2,425	16,006	14,644	1,405	2,982	19,031	13,106	1,507	4,109	18,722
7,113	8,874	2,401	945	12,220	14,052	3,244	749	18,045	12,640	2,822	2,527	17,989	13,197	2,998	4,558	20,753	6,951	805	8,522	16,278
..	482	..	..	482	128	..	..	128	..	..	..	..	95	..	1,176	1,271	..	..	1,530	1,530
11,784	13,568	2,286	2,302	18,156	25,172	4,710	1,844	31,726	16,326	2,523	6,245	25,094	19,698	3,160	8,668	31,526	13,288	2,009	8,837	24,734
5,442	36,601	10,135	6,344	53,080	41,310	10,873	8,677	60,860	28,384	6,022	10,061	44,467	36,690	6,256	11,1	54,056	25,635	3,109	12,362	41,106
43,858	65,533	17,180	5,415	88,128	81,266	18,103	12,472	111,840	39,508	6,722	15,179	61,409	40,610	7,999	14,20	62,815	34,220	6,689	22,055	63,864
1,030	31,249	5,015	13,679	49,943	34,607	5,818	24,115	64,540	33,956	3,994	44,021	81,971	49,560	4,935	63,77	118,269	40,808	4,149	80,856	125,813
..	1,683	..	379	2,062	1,009	..	343	1,352	107	36	..	143	2,218	194	..	2,412	800	..	71	871
..	3,509	46	..	3,555	7,076	39	..	7,115	3,017	37	..	3,054	2,017	..		2,521	597	254	505	1,356
7,044	465,290	75,952	100,721	581,963	495,300	89,605	112,615	697,520	285,533	43,743	150,696	479,972	348,944	53,150	200,769	602,863	251,219	37,880	274,784	563,883
7,501	3,516	..	549	4,065	4,322	..	760	5,082	7,604	..	1,551	9,155	7,712	..	2,420	10,132	792	..	122	914
15,446	9,804	..	2,483	12,287	10,290	..	2,542	12,832	10,744	..	2,756	13,500	18,874	..	4,462	23,336	15,998	..	4,004	20,002
358	..	..	376	376	..	..	363	363	..	..	304	304	..	..	329	329	..	..	259	259
23,306	13,320	..	3,408	16,728	14,612	..	3,665	18,277	18,348	..	4,011	22,959	26,586	..	7,211	33,797	16,790	..	4,385	21,175
9,313	9,118	..	1,073	10,191	8,520	..	1,805	10,325	9,874	..	3,383	13,257	5,602	..	4,507	10,109	345	..	4,323	4,633
2,105	4,253	..	1,142	5,394	7,745	..	2,960	10,705	955	..	489	1,444	714	..	235	949	..	..	372	372
2,507	1,826	..	680	2,506	1,955	..	..	1,955	1,592	..	3,966	5,558	1,813	..	2,829	4,042	2,384	..	2,894	5,273
..	2,571	..	..	2,571	2,069	..	1,052	3,121	2,892	..	1,654	4,546	3,421		1,133	4,554	8	..	347	355
1,702	2,028	..	..	2,028	3,522	..	..	3,522	3,355	..	1,946	5,301	1,013		2,161	3,174	..	..	179	179
..	470	..	..	470	844	..	..	844	2,314	..	..	2,314	4,449	..	1,052	5,501	103	..	..	103
15,627	20,265	..	2,895	23,160	24,655	..	5,817	30,472	20,982	..	11,438	32,420	17,012	..	11,917	28,929	2,840	..	8,115	10,955

No. III.—Statement showing the death-rate in districts affected by famine in 1896–97.

Province.	Average annual death-rate.	1896. October.	1896. November.	1896. December.	1897. January.	1897. February.	1897. March.	1897. April.	1897. May.	1897. June.	1897. July.	1897. August.
Madras.												
Kurnool	26·5	1·60	1·22	1·31	1·23	1·00	1·14	1·21	1·68	1·63	2·56	3·73
Cuddapah	22·6	1·41	1·34	1·78	1·75	1·29	1·23	1·28	1·74	1·44	1·59	1·88
Bellary	23·2	1·51	1·31	1·43	1·39	1·16	1·35	1·55	1·79	1·94	2·96	3·87
Anantapur	18·9	1·74	1·42	1·32	1·53	1·19	1·14	1·23	1·52	1·54	1·91	1·90
Ganjam	12·5	—	—	—	2·34	2·40	2·98	3·42	4·73	8·13	6·88	4·63
Vizagapatam	17·0	—	—	—	1·51	1·40	1·72	1·64	1·26	2·80	4·00	3·40
Bhadrachalam (Godavari District).	14·8	—	—	—	1·95	1·09	1·68	2·75	4·51	5·09	3·02	2·63
Bombay.												
Ahmednagar	36·28	2·20	2·13	2·12	1·92	1·77	2·07	2·63	3·32	3·50	6·86	7·18
Khandesh	33·79	2·64	2·34	2·36	2·26	1·99	2·52	3·00	2·95	3·17	3·62	7·32
Nasik	35·69	2·86	3·29	3·28	3·26	2·54	2·9	3·10	3·28	5·25	6·54	8·06
Poona	31·16	2·08	1·97	2·20	2·39	2·85	3·89	2·91	2·59	5·72	10·10	7·18
Satara	31·39	2·69	2·18	2·27	1·93	1·70	2·38	3·72	7·12	5·81	5·82	5·52
Sholapur	32·02	2·25	1·80	1·81	1·82	1·82	2·59	3·75	4·12	3·96	7·72	5·78
Belgaum	28·15	2·14	2·02	2·42	—	2·63	3·41	4·32	5·23	5·0	3·73	3·46
Bijapur	27·30	1·89	1·80	1·96	—	1·94	2·57	3·22	6·87	4·56	5·25	5·13
Dharwar	30·39	—	—	—	—	—	—	—	—	—	—	3·31
Bengal.												
Patna	32·12	2·41	2·11	1·93	1·50	1·36	(not reported.)	—	—	—	—	—
Shahabad	34·38	1·78	1·89	1·97	1·96	1·88	2·70	2·37	2·54	2·75	2·35	3·44
Saran	29·51	2·42	2·65	2·41	1·92	1·86	2·48	1·96	2·15	2·45	2·59	3·89
Champaran	32·64	2·91	3·22	2·84	2·20	2·36	3·03	2·15	2·40	2·44	2·49	4·50
Muzufferpore	33·40	3·68	2·59	2·37	1·83	1·90	2·61	1·99	2·20	2·26	2·62	4·07
Darbhanga	20·07	2·4	2·3	3·1	1·6	1·4	2·2	1·8	2·06	2·1	2·0	2·9
Palamau	33·50	2·49	2·44	2·19	1·75	1·73	2·14	1·73	2·43	3·43	4·62	6·43
Manbhum	24·09	1·19	1·51	1·95	1·41	1·4	2·46	2·09	3·27	3·96	4·08	4·49
Hazaribagh	31·19	2·31	2·49	2·54	1·77	1·72	2·44	2·18	2·86	3·03	5·34	10·51
Lohardaga	27·65	2·36	2·04	2·26	1·64	1·69	2·19	1·61	1·9	1·97	3·42	12·07
Nadia	38·03	1·99	2·34	2·46	1·87	1·91	3·15	3·37	2·44	1·70	1·64	1·83
Khulna	29·05	2·78	3·79	3·69	3·12	2·30	3·41	2·74	2·01	1·59	1·86	2·38
Puri	29·82	1·30	1·53	2·23	2·49	2·07	2·68	2·36	2·98	5·58	4·87	4·66
Bhagalpur	32·80	2·1	2·1	2·07	1·7	1·6	2·2	—	2·1	2·1	2·29	3·5
Sonthal Parganas	20·92	1·45	1·40	1·44	1·13	1·02	1·67	1·71	1·86	2·43	2·85	4·13
Murshidabad	33·91	—	—	—	1·85	1·82	2·75	2·55	2·71	2·12	2·61	2·74
Bankura	24·15	—	—	—	—	—	—	—	2·87	2·47	2·44	1·92
North-Western Provinces and Oudh (distressed districts).												
Agra	28·90	2·34	2·23	2·31	2·11	1·72	1·95	2·05	2·61	2·94	2·63	4·17
Etawah	28·58	2·43	2·14	2·38	2·71	2·01	2·22	2·65	2·80	2·61	2·20	3·08
Cawnpore	33·73	2·59	2·37	2·82	2·86	2·47	2·77	2·90	2·83	2·62	2·70	2·81
Lalitpur	34·37* 34·44	—	—	—	—	4·84	—	—	—	—	—	—
Fatehpur	34·55	2·26	2·80	4·66	6·36	—	6·83	4·55	4·03	3·01	2·68	2·93
Banda	30·02	4·20	4·39	4·71	5·10	4·81	5·09	5·23	4·73	3·60	2·62	2·61
Hamirpur	37·35	8·06	6·13	5·35	5·03	3·64	3·41	2·15	2·97	4·07	3·80	6·62
Allahabad	30·75	2·37	2·08	3·34	3·55	3·48	5·40	4·41	2·98	3·09	2·45	2·70
Jhansi	31·43	7·37	5·86	5·29	4·92	4·16	3·73	2·59	2·73	3·25	3·18	4·40
Jalaun	35·25	3·24	3·01	3·29	3·29	2·75	3·09	2·62	2·59	3·67	4·39	6·19
Mirzapur	33·06	2·54	2·23	2·95	4·04	3·80	4·86	4·82	3·97	3·45	3·83	4·57
Jaunpur	30·12	1·65	1·84	2·22	2·30	2·25	3·23	3·86	3·15	2·48	2·83	3·18
Gorakhpur	30·08	2·52	2·38	2·82	3·26	2·84	2·69	2·57	2·11	2·10	3·20	4·09
Azamgarh	31·43	1·60	1·84	2·32	2·97	2·75	2·71	2·62	2·26	2·34	3·89	5·02
Lucknow	36·18	2·01	2·25	3·20	3·87	3·33	3·80	3·91	3·41	3·06	4·89	6·00
Unao	30·74	1·96	1·73	2·59	3·63	3·31	3·86	3·52	3·08	2·34	2·81	3·26
Rai Bareli	33·93	2·01	2·37	3·71	4·81	4·38	5·42	5·21	4·01	2·95	2·94	3·64
Sitapur	31·94	2·90	2·63	2·61	2·52	2·30	2·49	3·68	3·39	2·96	2·70	3·11
Hardoi	31·77	4·43	2·76	3·49	4·39	4·0	4·71	5·27	3·51	2·95	4·37	5·72
Bara Banki	35·88	1·74	1·66	2·13	2·15	1·95	2·54	3·11	3·36	2·87	3·22	3·34

* Town Circle 34·37, Rural „ 34·44 } Lalitpur is included in the figures given for Jhansi.

No. III.—Statement showing the death-rate in districts affected by famine in 1896–97—*cont.*

Province.	Average annual death-rate.	1896. October.	1896. November.	1896. December.	1897. January.	1897. February.	1897. March.	1897. April.	1897. May.	1897. June.	1897. July.	1897. August.
Districts slightly distressed.												
Dehra Dun	27·16	2·85	2·40	2·09	2·29	1·85	1·69	2·04	2·40	1·77	—	—
Muttra	20·83	2·27	2·29	2·17	1·83	1·29	1·31	1·75	1·78	2·37	1·73	2·06
Farukhabad	34·01	2·88	2·50	2·81	2·89	2·69	3·26	3·72	3·44	2·60	2·55	2·78
Mainpuri	23·00	2·10	2·27	2·67	2·39	1·90	2·02	2·39	2·21	1·98	1·65	1·80
Etah	27·53	2·83	2·54	2·22	2·53	2·38	2·75	3·25	3·01	2·57	2·48	2·59
Bareilly	32·11	8·33	6·07	4·55	2·85	2·90	2·48	3·01	2·78	2·15	2·10	2·63
Bijnor	37·14	4·47	3·53	3·51	3·48	2·36	3·32	3·78	3·82	2·22	1·93	2·30
Budaun	27·39	3·45	2·80	3·35	3·52	3·19	2·53	3·82	2·85	2·22	2·21	2·46
Moradabad	37·19	6·90	4·14	3·54	3·33	2·59	2·84	2·88	3·04	1·96	1·95	2·62
Shahjahanpur	35·01	7·59	4·28	3·80	3·37	3·00	3·69	3·69	3·02	2·20	2·35	3·93
Pilibhit	35·44	9·10	7·16	4·81	3·00	2·02	2·22	2·75	2·31	1·88	1·96	2·27
Benares	33·10	2·63	2·28	2·64	2·61	2·48	3·15	3·57	3·27	3·21	3·76	4·39
Basti	31·55	2·19	2·17	2·74	2·55	2·65	2·62	2·95	2·35	2·50	2·80	2·59
Kheri	38·44	4·76	3·60	2·94	2·57	2·16	2·53	3·47	3·23	2·47	2·50	2·95
Fyzabad	31·54	2·22	2·75	2·95	2·93	2·35	2·59	2·39	2·20	1·81	2·70	3·39
Gonda	34·94	2·58	2·91	3·31	3·33	3·20	4·32	4·03	3·72	3·13	3·77	4·84
Sultanpur	35·61	1·88	2·17	2·93	3·19	3·27	3·07	4·62	3·59	2·41	2·57	2·82
Partabgarh	29·74	2·09	1·83	2·70	3·21	3·84	4·80	4·23	3·66	2·32	2·16	12·59
Punjab.												
Hissar	30·3	2·33	2·25	2·25	2·13	1·75	1·90	2·43	3·03	3·34	3·35	2·25
Rohtak	29·3	2·25	2·58	2·25	2·12	1·59	1·51	1·73	2·10	2·41	2·33	2·17
Gurgaon	32·0	2·75	2·75	2·42	2·16	1·56	1·54	1·79	2·21	—	—	—
Delhi	40·1	2·17	2·50	2·75	1·83	1·70	1·77	2·02	2·47	2·43	1·99	2·5
Karnal	38·8	2·25	3·17	2·42	2·26	1·79	1·85	1·99	2·41	2·70	2·56	2·88
Umballa	40·6	3·08	3·08	3·00	2·44	2·22	1·87	1·89	1·90	1·77	1·90	2·33
Ferozepore	30·8	1·83	1·91	1·83	1·48	1·77	2·16	2·07	2·28	2·34	2·08	—
Lahore	36·2	2·17	2·33	2·42	1·66	1·72	1·06	1·59	—	—	—	—
Gujrat	29·0	2·00	1·83	1·58	2·18	1·52	1·35	1·52	1·66	1·49	—	—
Burma.												
Meiktila	—	—	—	—		1·00	3·50	3·50	3·50	3·00	3·00	2·5
Yamethim	—	—	—	—	not reported.	0·98	4·18	3·37	3·35	1·73	1·98	1·76
Myingyan	—	—	—	—		0·88	1·36	2·72	2·26	2·04	2·37	1·68
Central Provinces.												
Saugor	39·33	8·1	6·3	5·6	5·3	4·9	4·2	5·6	7·48	10·37	8·26	11·26
Damoh	37·93	1·02	7·8	5·8	5·5	4·3	3·4	4·9	6·01	6·39	4·57	7·36
Jabalpur	36·90	7·4	5·0	4·9	6·9	6·9	7·7	5·4	6·31	5·71	4·38	5·60
Narsingpore	41·26	7·7	5·7	5·1	6·5	4·0	4·0	8·2	7·41	6·48	6·26	7·24
Hoshangabad	39·18	4·6	3·8	4·4	4·2	3·2	2·9	2·9	7·76	6·15	4·33	6·95
Nimar	43·73	4·4	4·2	4·2	3·9	3·3	3·3	3·9	5·39	6·96	5·60	7·32
Mandla	31·53	6·0	3·5	4·0	3·9	7·1	6·7	4·2	7·17	10·52	16·44	16·66
Betul	36·21	3·5	3·0	3·1	3·6	3·5	4·8	4·3	3·63	6·30	7·45	11·76
Chhindwara	34·16	3·4	3·2	3·0	2·5	2·1	2·5	2·6	2·83	4·08	4·46	4·80
Seoni	30·60	6·1	4·2	4·6	5·3	4·4	4·4	4·2	4·62	6·86	8·28	12·29
Balaghat	30·50	6·2	4·3	5·2	4·9	4·5	6·7	4·0	6·56	11·76	8·81	11·75
Bhandara	31·40	4·3	3·8	3·5	3·5	2·6	2·9	2·8	4·47	7·02	5·48	6·42
Nagpur	31·60	3·1	2·5	2·5	2·2	1·8	2·0	2·7	4·54	4·83	3·93	5·68
Wardha	38·00	3·5	2·6	2·5	2·1	1·7	2·0	2·6	4·22	5·59	4·00	6·24
Chanda	31·46	2·8	2·3	2·1	2·0	1·7	0·9	—	2·55	2·83	3·30	4·17
Raipur	31·98	4·0	3·2	3·0	2·7	2·2	2·9	4·1	7·50	9·05	7·16	9·66
Bilaspur	28·30	3·8	3·3	3·4	3·1	3·9	5·2	6·7	6·79	10·99	9·02	12·51
Sambalpur	28·51	1·9	1·6	2·1	2·3	1·9	1·4	2·8	3·01	4·11	2·30	3·78
Berar.												
Amraoti	38·9	3·5	2·8	2·7	2·4	2·1	2·5	3·6	5·5	3·3	3·9	8·0
Akola	40·8	3·0	2·3	2·3	2·0	2·0	1·7	2·4	4·04	4·8	4·7	11·2
Ellichpur	42·8	3·2	2·5	2·5	2·1	—	—	—	—	—	—	—
Wun	33·0	2·8	1·9	2·0	1·7	1·7	1·9	2·4	3·2	3·1	—	5·7
Basim	37·7	3·1	2·1	2·0	1·7	1·5	1·8	1·9	2·3	2·8	3·8	7·8
Buldana	40·7	3·4	2·3	2·1	2·0	1·65	1·76	1·9	2·44	2·4	3·1	5·26

No. IV.—Statement showing the number of deaths from all causes registered in each province from August 1896 to July 1897.

Province.	August.	September.	October.	November.	December.	January.	February.	March.	April.	May.	June.	July.	TOTAL.
Madras.													
1896-67	59,052	59,694	59,602	60,417	79,213	76,115	53,362	52,259	48,542	54,876	59,074	75,543	737,749
Average	*59,463*	*56,353*	*54,953*	*57,697*	*70,205*	*66,325*	*51,527*	*50,900*	*47,720*	*51,421*	*50,425*	*57,747*	*674,796*
Bombay.													
1896-97	58,903	44,082	40,961	41,040	46,722	50,833	47,549	54,353	56,506	59,827	60,611	75,782	637,169
Average	*55,081*	*46,905*	*46,236*	*48,728*	*47,043*	*46,801*	*43,335*	*47,519*	*48,370*	*50,953*	*46,918*	*58,120*	*584,009*
Bengal.													
1896-97	183,902	163,738	151,392	194,405	214,759	154,095	140,493	211,392	189,410	175,987	162,550	171,842	2,113,965
Average	*176,486*	*163,462*	*196,919*	*225,393*	*244,901*	*190,816*	*154,257*	*188,502*	*196,978*	*177,479*	*160,857*	*165,274*	*2,241,364*
North-Western Provinces and Oudh.													
1896-97	131,837	140,611	144,754	126,699	141,406	143,956	125,975	145,830	149,863	135,532	120,859	130,244	1,637,566
Average	*127,598*	*135,118*	*153,561*	*148,542*	*146,621*	*119,221*	*99,109*	*109,463*	*124,208*	*135,124*	*114,995*	*111,717*	*1,525,277*
Punjab.													
1896-97	47,639	51,611	52,468	51,084	50,453	44,262	34,550	36,492	35,695	41,928	41,672	38,907	526,761
Average	*47,490*	*65,106*	*91,869*	*79,966*	*69,395*	*62,920*	*46,897*	*43,762*	*41,484*	*51,084*	*45,940*	*40,637*	*686,550*
Central Provinces.													
1896-97	50,098	47,196	46,190	35,977	35,348	36,547	31,153	32,708	38,362	56,318	56,944	61,445	528,286
Average	*34,406*	*35,481*	*35,343*	*31,285*	*29,189*	*25,548*	*24,265*	*27,666*	*31,245*	*36,115*	*32,205*	*32,853*	*375,801*
Berar.													
1896-97	11,796	10,839	9,104	6,832	6,514	5,856	5,002	5,682	7,839	11,125	10,368	13,188	104,145
Average	*12,050*	*12,010*	*11,019*	*9,439*	*8,256*	*7,427*	*6,936*	*9,533*	*10,701*	*10,511*	*7,322*	*10,001*	*115,214*

NOTE.—The "average" here given is the average number of deaths for the month during the preceding five years.

No. V.—*Statement showing the number of units of relief (of one day each) relieved in each Province and in Native States.*

Province.	October 1896.	November 1896.	December 1896.	January 1897.	February 1897.	March 1897.	April 1897.	May 1897.	June 1897.	July 1897.	August 1897.	September 1897.	Total.
Madras	...	554,000	897,000	926,000	1,602,000	3,091,000	5,032,000	9,105,000	18,176,000	22,048,000	18,827,000	12,217,000	92,475,000
Bombay	...	160,000	2,975,000	7,362,000	10,744,000	15,073,000	12,184,000	10,359,000	17,381,000	10 896,000	11,534,000	15,312,000	113,980,000
Bengal	...	68,000	1,417,000	7,675,000	11,340,000	17,423,000	18,267,000	22,069,000	27,795,000	17,132,000	11,640,000	3,672,000	138,493,000
North-Western Provinces and Oudh	634,000	3,452,000	17,160,000	26,346,000	43,428,000	42,593,000	30,774,000	38,850,000	40,473,000	19,147,000	12,302,000	8,535,000	283,694,000
Punjab	180,000	234,000	819,000	2,180,000	3,201,000	4,008,000	2,480,000	2,584,000	3,449,000	1,535,000	661,000	237,000	21,568,000
Central Provinces	...	...	2,105,000	6,383,000	9,082,000	13,725,000	14,061,000	18,555,000	19,842,000	16,114,000	16,198,000	22,092,000	138,157,000
Burma	60,000	378,000	1,051,000	877,000	812,000	835,000	458,000	457,000	557,000	808,000	766,000	634,000	7,693,000
Berar	...	...	...	...	206,000	616,000	513,000	811,000	969,000	849,000	412,000	291,000	4,667,000
Total	874,000	4,841,000	26,424,000	51,749,000	80,415,000	97,364,000	83,769,000	102,790,000	128,642,000	88,529,000	72,340,000	62,990,000	800,727,000
NATIVE STATES.													
Central India	436,000	178,000	524,000	1,314,000	3,083,000	4,199,000	4,211,000	4,598,000	5,809,000	2,352,000	1,414,000	1,170,000	29,288,000
Hyderabad	...	...	...	...	49,000	140,000	492,000	806,000	724,000	412,000	561,000	790,000	3,974,000
Rajputana	158,000	573,000	1,279,000	795,000	616,000	1,037,000	703,000	625,000	847,000	463,000	224,000	184,000	7,504,000
Total	594,000	751,000	1,803,000	2,109,000	3,748,000	5,876,000	5,406,000	6,029,000	7,380,000	3,227,000	2,199,000	2,144,000	40,766,000
GRAND TOTAL	1,468,000	5,592,000	28,227,000	53,858,000	84,163,000	102,740,000	89,175,000	108,819,000	136,022,000	91,756,000	74,539,000	65,134,000	841,493,000
Number of weeks included in each month.	5 26th September to 31st October.	4 1st November to 28th November.	5 29th November to 2nd January.	4 3rd January to 30th January.	4 31st January to 27th February.	5 28th February to 3rd April.	4 4th April to 1st May.	4 2nd May to 29th May.	5 30th May to 3rd July.	4 4th July to 31st July.	4 1st August to 28th August.	5 29th August to 2nd October.	
Average number receiving relief during month.													
(1) British India	25,000	173,000	755,000	1,848,000	2,871,000	2,782,000	2,991,000	3,670,000	3,676,000	3,161,000	2,583,000	1,799,000	
(2) Native States	17,000	27,000	51,000	75,000	133,000	154,000	193,000	215,000	211,000	115,000	78,000	61,000	
(3) British India and Native States	42,000	300,000	806,000	1,923,000	3,004,000	2,936,000	3,184,000	3,885,000	3,887,000	3,276,000	2,661,000	1,860,000	

No. VI.—*Statement showing the average number of persons receiving relief in each month in each Province and in Native States.*

Province.	October 1896.	November 1896.	December 1896.	January 1897.	February 1897.	March 1897.	April 1897.	May 1897.	June 1897.	July 1897.	August 1897.	September 1897.
Madras	—	20,000	26,000	33,000	57,000	88,000	180,000	325,000	519,000	787,000	672,000	349,000
Bombay	—	6,000	85,000	263,000	384,000	431,000	435,000	370,000	497,000	389,000	412,000	437,000
Bengal	—	2,000	40,000	274,000	405,000	498,000	652,000	788,000	794,000	612,000	416,000	105,000
North-Western Provinces and Oudh	18,000	123,000	490,000	941,000	1,551,000	1,217,000	1,099,000	1,387,000	1,156,000	684,000	439,000	244,000
Punjab	5,000	9,000	24,000	78,000	114,000	114,000	89,000	92,000	99,000	55,000	24,000	7,000
Central Provinces	—	—	60,000	228,000	324,000	392,000	502,000	663,000	567,000	575,000	578,000	631,000
Burma	2,000	13,000	30,000	31,000	29,000	24,000	16,000	16,000	16,000	29,000	27,000	18,000
Berar	—	—	—	—	7,000	18,000	18,000	29,000	28,000	30,000	15,000	8,000
Total	25,000	173,000	755,000	1,848,000	2,871,000	2,782,000	2,991,000	3,670,000	3,676,000	3,161,000	2,583,000	1,799,000
Native States.												
Central India	12,000	6,000	15,000	47,000	110,000	120,000	150,000	164,000	166,000	84,000	50,000	33,000
Hyderabad	—	—	—	—	1,000	4,000	18,000	29,000	21,000	15,000	20,000	23,000
Rajputana	5,000	21,000	36,000	28,000	22,000	30,000	25,000	22,000	24,000	16,000	8,000	5,000
Total	17,000	27,000	51,000	75,000	133,000	154,000	193,000	215,000	211,000	115,000	78,000	61,000
GRAND TOTAL	42,000	300,000	806,000	1,923,000	3,004,000	2,936,000	3,184,000	3,885,000	3,887,000	3,276,000	2,661,000	1,860,000

No. VII.—Statement showing the net imports and exports of food-grains from January to September 1897.

(Tons.)

[Net imports +]. [Net exports —].

—		November to December 1896.	January to March 1897.	April to June.	July to September.	Total.
Principal Ports.						
Calcutta ...	...	+ 4,618	+ 44,334	+ 122,056	+ 74,409	+ 245,417
Rangoon...	...	— 90,754	— 517,019	— 269,320	— 170,225	— 1,047,318
Madras ...	...	+ 1,305	+ 8,687	+ 14,323	+ 13,030	+ 37,345
Bombay ...	...	+ 41,374	+ 31,820	+ 60,359	+ 86,213	+ 219,766
Karachi ...	...	— 21,517	— 14,950	— 26,482	— 39,167	— 102,116
Provinces and Districts.	*Bengal—*		*From 17th January, 1897.*			
Division.	**District.**					
Patna ...	Patna ...	...	+ 1,840	+ 1,991	+ 10,789	+ 14,620
	Gaya ...	...	— 1,888	+ 3,747	+ 5,617	+ 7,476
	Shahabad ...	...	+ 1,040	— 4,324	+ 3,504	+ 220
	Saran ...	...	+ 11,318	+ 18,044	+ 14,779	+ 44,141
	Champaran ...	...	+ 5,551	+ 8,240	+ 1,598	+ 15,389
	Muzaffarpur ...	...	+ 6,272	+ 17,428	+ 9,164	+ 32,864
	Darbhanga ...	...	+ 4,621	+ 26,416	+ 13.438	+ 44,475
Bhagalpur ...	Monghyr ...	...	— 18,069	— 7,950	— 5,037	— 31,056
	Bhagalpur ...	...	— 14,978	— 4,473	— 8,103	— 27,554
	Purnea ...	...	— 731	— 1,287	— 22	— 2,040
	Malda ...	...	— 26	— 7	+ 40	+ 7
	Sonthal Parganas ...	...	— 8,214	— 1,197	+ 1,400	— 8,011
Rajshahi ...	Rajshahi ...	...	+ 5,573	+ 5,084	+ 1,260	+ 11,917
	Dinajpur ...	...	— 7,920	— 4,930	+ 23	— 12,827
	Jalpaiguri ...	...	+ 3,028	+ 5,148	+ 4,523	+ 12,699
	Darjeeling ...	...	+ 1,793	+ 2,171	+ 1,965	+ 5,929
	Rangpur ...	...	— 408	+ 433	— 889	— 864
	Bogra ...	...	— 5,631	— 4,632	+ 1,712	— 8,551
	Pabna ...	...	+ 3,894	+ 4,864	+ 702	+ 9,460
Dacca ...	Dacca ...	...	— 173	+ 15	+ 334	+ 176
	Narainganj ...	...	— 4,772	— 125	+ 151	— 4,746
	Maimensingh ...	...	+ 2,406	+ 106	+ 251	+ 2,763
	Faridpur ...	...	— 4	+ 1,076	+ 1,866	+ 2,938
	Backerganj ...	...	— 470	— 746	— 452	— 1,668

Note.—In the case of the *ports* the figures include imports and exports by rail and sea.
In the case of *districts* the figures as a rule are for rail borne traffic only, but in certain cases (such as Chittagong or Balasore) they include coasting traffic.
The figures are *net*: that is, the imports have been deducted from the exports, or *vice versâ*.
As the imports of one district are the exports of another, no inference as to the gross volume of trade can be made by taking the aggregate totals. Only districts on the line of rail are shown.

Net Imports and Exports of food-grains—contd.

(Tons.)

[Net imports +].

[Net exports —].

Division.	District.	17th January to March 1897.	April to June.	July to September.	Total.
Chittagong ...	Tippera	— 444	+ 123	+ 610	+ 289
	Noakhali	— 92	— 121	— 15	— 228
	Chittagong	+ 4,132	+ 7,536	+ 5,701	+ 17,369
Burdwan ...	Burdwan	+ 23,022	— 23,900	— 14,036	— 60,958
	Birbhum	— 35,600	— 14,106	— 9,602	— 59,308
	Hooghly	+ 786	+ 96	+ 345	+ 1,227
	Midnapur	— 8,643*	— 30,860	...	— 39,503
Presidency ...	24-Parganas	+ 51	— 40	+ 279	+ 290
	Nadia	— 5,804	+ 4,522	— 404	— 1,686
	Murshidabad	— 4,504	— 2,645	— 1,539	— 8,688
	Jessore	+ 2,421	+ 3,369	+ 1,580	+ 7,370
	Khulna	— 827	+ 11	+ 154	— 662
Chota Nagpur ...	Hazaribagh	+ 2,538	+ 3,648	+ 1,216	+ 7,402
	Lohardaga	+ 18	...	...	+ 18
	Manbhum	+ 1,796	+ 2,931	+ 2,814	+ 7,541
	Singhbhum	— 830	— 708	+ 77	— 1,461
	Ranchi	— 138	+ 8	+ 20	— 110
Orissa	Cuttack	— 3,971	— 6,287	— 2,058	— 12,316
	Balasore	— 13,709	— 16,321	— 12,791	— 42,821
	Puri	— 117	— 931	— 897	— 1,945
North-Western Provinces—					
Meerut ...	Saharanpur	+ 3,684	— 667	— 1,122	+ 1,895
	Muzaffarnagar ...	+ 5,194	— 10,455	— 4,507	— 9,768
	Meerut	+ 5,786	— 9,780	— 7,490	— 11,484
	Bulandshahr	— 327	— 14,782	— 12,908	— 28,017
	Aligarh	+ 1,517	— 11,777	— 16,222	— 26,482
Agra	Muttra	+ 1,852	— 2,608	— 2,075	— 2,831
	Agra	+ 3,317	+ 2,267	— 4,746	+ 838
	Farukhabad	+ 2,333	+ 738	+ 235	+ 3,306

* For March 1897.

Net Imports and Exports of food-grains—contd.

(Tons.)

[Net imports +]

[Net exports —].

Division.	District.	17th January to March 1897.	April to June.	July to September.	Total.
	Mainpuri	+ 573	— 533	— 496	— 456
	Etawah	+ 885	+ 371	— 617	+ 639
	Etah	+ 48	— 4,140	— 3,130	— 7,222
Rohilkhand ...	Bijnor	+ 3,453	+ 1,914	+ 2,858	+ 8,225
	Moradabad	+ 3,615	— 9,162	— 2,311	— 7,858
	Shahjahánpur ..	+ 1,444	— 9,006	— 560	— 8,122
	Budaun	+ 33	— 584	— 110	— 661
	Pilibít	+ 1,440	— 2,328	— 51	— 939
	Bareli	+ 1,455	— 2,634	+ 217	— 962
Allahabad ...	Cawnpore	+ 18,030	+ 24,627	+ 2,314	+ 44,971
	Fatehpur	+ 2,064	+ 3,262	+ 2,823	+ 8,149
	Bánda	+ 5,250	+ 13,151	+ 5,172	+ 23,573
	Hamirpur	+ 893	+ 2,509	+ 2,042	+ 5,444
	Allahabad	+ 21,273	+ 13,136	+ 11,120	+ 45,529
	Jhansi	+ 2,649	+ 9,867	+ 4,607	+ 17,123
	Jalaun	+ 808	+ 4,794	+ 4,063	+ 9,665
Benares ...	Benares	+ 4,250	+ 11,994	+ 6,362	+ 22,606
	Mirzapur	+ 1,445	+ 4,786	+ 2,312	+ 8,543
	Jaunpur	+ 2,972	+ 1,279	+ 2,377	+ 6,628
	Ghazipur	+ 845	+ 342	+ 1,602	+ 2,789
Gorakhpur ...	Basti	— 661	— 6,781	— 4,831	— 12,273
	Ballia	+ 375	+ 82	+ 146	+ 603
	Gorakhpur	— 92	— 12,868	— 1,458	— 14,418
Kumaun ...	Garhwal	+ 37	+ 162	+ 48	+ 247
	Naini Tal	— 915	— 1,348	+ 198	— 2,065
Oudh—					
Lucknow ...	Lucknow	+ 3,982	+ 6,348	+ 5,683	+ 16,013
	Unao	+ 1,910	+ 59	+ 294	+ 2,263
	Rae-Bareli	+ 5,198	+ 1,595	+ 2,854	+ 9,647

Net Imports and Exports of food-grains—contd.

(Tons.)

[Net imports +].

[Net exports —].

Division	District	17th January to March 1897.	April to June.	July to September.	Total.
DIVISION.	DISTRICT.				
	Sitapur	— 1,242	— 8,346	— 4,765	— 14,353
	Kheri ...	— 1,168	— 3,460	— 1,216	— 5,844
	Hardoi	+ 3,651	— 514	+ 1,109	+ 4,246
Fyzabad ...	Fyzabad	+ 937	— 3,651	— 819	— 3,533
	Gonda	+ 2,476	— 1,245	— 1,156	+ 75
	Bahraich	— 379	— 5,576	— 1,513	— 7,468
	Barabanki	— 2,009	— 2,976	— 4,368	— 9,353
Rajputana—					
Jodhpur ...	... ...	...	— 2,372	— 916	— 3,288
Bikaner ..	... ...	...	+ 3,922	+ 3,823	+ 7,745
Ajmere-Merwara	... ...	+ 687	+ 3,458	+ 4,449	+ 8,594
Punjab—					
Delhi ...	Hissar	+ 9,830	+ 20,248	+ 5,907	+ 35,985
	Rohtak	— 22	+ 70	+ 37	+ 85
	Gurgaon	+ 1,201	— 2,792	— 2,502	— 4,093
	Delhi	+ 9,735	+ 7,453	— 1,473	+ 15,715
	Karnal	+ 1,198	— 1,142	— 14	+ 42
	Ambala	+ 4,640	+ 4,757	+ 3,751	+ 13,148
	Simla	+ 602	+ 1,411	+ 698	+ 2,711
Jalandhar ...	Jalandhar	— 3,567	— 18,199	— 8,372	— 30,138
	Ludhiana	— 8,342	— 7,711	— 8,166	— 24,219
	Ferozepur	— 8,420	— 4,757	— 4,640	— 17,817
Lahore	Multan	+ 2,289	— 1,429	— 1,245	— 385
	Jhang	+ 547	— 3,824	— 2,226	— 5,503
	Montgomery	+ 2,652	+ 301	+ 217	+ 3,170
	Lahore	+ 7,594	— 4,091	— 696	+ 2,807
	Amritsar	+ 838	— 8,938	— 2,436	— 10,536
	Gurdaspur	— 1,272	— 9,272	— 2,869	— 13,413
Rawalpindi ...	Sialkot	— 147	+ 1,763	+ 1,234	+ 2,850

Net Imports and Exports of food-grains—contd.

(Tons.)

[Net imports +].

[Net exports —].

		17th January to March 1897.	April to June.	July to September.	Total.
DIVISION.	**DISTRICT.**				
	Gujrat	+ 3,204	+ 110	+ 918	+ 4,232
	Gujranwala	+ 1,855	+ 12,200	— 5,007	— 15,352
	Shahpur	+ 1,330	— 1,139	— 382	— 191
	Jhelam	+ 4,278	— 1,407	+ 1,239	+ 6,924
	Rawalpindi	+ 7,022	+ 15,609	+ 12,141	+ 34,772
Peshawar ...	Peshawar	— 713	+ 1,958	— 3,082	— 1,837
Derajat ...	Bannu	— 1,576	— 1,616	— 1,091	— 4,283
	Dera Ismail Khan ...	— 1,804	— 2,373	— 3,457	— 7,634
	Muzaffargarh... ...	— 933	— 2,662	— 2,114	— 5,709
Bombay Presidency—					
Guzerat ...	Ahmadabad	+ 1,267	+ 5,110	+ 2,046	+ 8,423
	Kaira	— 1,458	+ 478	+ 1,502	+ 522
	Panch Mahals ...	— 9,288	— 11,668	— 2,443	— 23,399
	Broach	+ 3,218	+ 76	+ 511	+ 3,805
	Surat	+ 3,868	+ 8,945	+ 3,501	+ 16,314
	Bhavnagar	+ 2,576	...	...	+ 2,576
	Kathiawar	+ 658	+ 5,527	+ 744	+ 6,929
Deccan ...	Khandesh	+ 8,181	+ 14,113	+ 15,487	+ 37,781
	Nasik	+ 3,479	+ 7,578	+ 10,907	+ 21,964
	Ahmadnagar	+ 1,190	+ 1,484	+ 6,469	+ 9,143
	Poona	+ 7,668	+ 16,843	+ 14,161	+ 38,672
	Sholapur	+ 790	— 1,844	+ 11,090	+ 10,036
	Satara	+ 4,409	+ 6,610	+ 10,922	+ 21,941
Karnatak ...	Belgaum	— 779	+ 7,722	+ 6,594	+ 13,537
	Bijapur	+ 4,397	+ 5,102	+ 16,013	+ 25,512
	Dharwar	— 4,026	— 5,940	— 3,273	— 13,239
	Tanna	— 3,314	— 1,164	— 422	— 4,900
	Kolaba	— 918	+ 225	+ 275	— 418
	Kolhapur	+ 5,450	+ 12,539	+ 9,264	+ 27,253

Net Imports and Exports of food-grains—contd.

(Tons.)

[Net imports +].

[Net exports —].

		17th January to March 1897.	April to June.	July to September.	Total.
DIVISION.	DISTRICT.				
	Kanara	— 2,006	— 1,591	— 48	— 3,645
	Ratnagiri	+ 6,767	+ 16,938	+ 1,084	+ 24,789
Sind and Baluchistan—					
Shikarpur ...	... ...	— 17,382	— 29,978	— 27,052	— 74,412
Thar-Parkar ...	... ...	— 316	— 1,275	+ 2,303	+ 712
Upper Sind Frontier	... ...	— 4,537	— 3,009	— 3,031	— 10,577
Hyderabad ...	... ...	+ 228	— 1,330	— 2,630	— 3,732
Central Provinces—					
Jubbulpur ...	Saugor	— 169	+ 7,211	+ 5,023	+ 12,065
	Jubbulpur	— 360	+ 4,691	+ 2,142	+ 6,473
Nerbudda ...	Narsinghpur	— 1,322	+ 2,641	+ 2,770	+ 4,089
	Hoshangabad... ...	+ 588	+ 4,878	+ 2,553	+ 8,019
	Nimar	+ 2,296	+ 2,524	+ 4,085	+ 8,905
Nagpur ...	Wardha	+ 977	+ 720	+ 1,745	+ 3,442
	Nagpur	+ 3,839	+ 8,629	+ 4,897	+ 17,365
	Chanda	— 562	— 1,106	— 356	— 2,024
	Bhandara	+ 771	+ 7,678	+ 2,274	+ 10,723
Chattisgarh ...	Raipur	— 10,763	— 2,597	— 977	— 14,337
	Bilaspur	+ 36	+ 2,604	+ 2,843	+ 5,483
	Sambalpur	— 9,184	— 7,376	— 6,039	— 22,599
Berar—					
East—					
Amraoti ...	... ...	+ 3,670	+ 2,917	+ 5,815	+ 12,402
West—					
Akola	... ...	+ 1,587	— 672	+ 3,850	+ 4,765
Buldana ...	... ...	+ 643	+ 485	+ 601	+ 1,729
Madras—					
Ganjam ...	... ...	— 992	— 1,679	+ 4,647	+ 1,976
Vizagapatam ...	... ...	+ 3,780	+ 6,991	+ 10,293	+ 21,064

Net Imports and Exports of food-grains—contd.

(Tons.)

[Net imports +].

[Net exports —].

DIVISION.	DISTRICT.	17th January to March 1897.	April to June.	July to September.	Total.
Godavari	... ...	— 9,184	— 21,611	— 22,181	— 52,976
Kistna	... ...	— 9,044	— 17,193	— 17,049	— 43,286
Nellore	... ...	— 367	— 517	— 1,495	— 2,379
Karnul	... ...	+ 984	+ 661	+ 1,756	+ 3,401
Bellary	... ...	+ 2,171	+ 4,092	+ 10,686	+ 16,949
Anantapur	... ...	+ 59	— 1,686	+ 165	— 1,462
Cuddapah	... ...	+ 1,374	— 591	— 66	— 717
North Arcot	... ...	— 1,110	— 5,936	— 5,602	— 12,648
Chingleput	... ...	— 1,565	— 3,827	— 5,058	— 10,450
South Arcot	... ...	— 4,930	— 14,756	— 16,093	— 35,779
Salem	... ...	— 2,399	— 4,944	— 9,404	— 16,747
Coimbatore	... ...	— 7,667	— 7,556	— 7,446	— 22,669
Trichinopoly	... ...	— 1,748	— 2,436	— 5,920	— 10,104
Tanjore	... ...	— 30,901	— 64,135	— 48,464	— 143,500
Madura	... ...	— 3,530	— 7,531	— 9,364	— 20,425
Tinnevelly	... ...	+ 239	+ 2,340	+ 2,362	+ 4,941
Malabar	... ...	+ 16,230	+ 23,672	+ 12,633	+ 52,535
South Canara	... .	— 12,662	— 6,193	— 88	— 18,943

No. VIII. Statement showing extension of irrigation from State Irrigation Works in India since 1881.

Year.	Areas irrigated from all classes of works in						
	Madras.	Bombay.		Bengal.	North-Western Provinces.	Punjab	Total.
		Deccan and Gujarat	Sind.				
	Acres.	Acres.	Acres.	Acres.	Acres.	Acres.	Acres.
1881–82 ...	5,653,197	160,658	1,601,986	415,453	1,915,949	1,687,725	11,443,968
1882–83 ...	5,949,801	167,004	1,673,293	410,532	1,974,175	1,683,272	11,858,077
1883–84 ...	5,496,595	171,430	1,540,831	518,414	2,297,674	1,652,068	11,677,012
1884–85 ...	5,173,724	180,290	1,783,173	519,550	1,617,304	1,614,288	10,888,329
1885–86 ...	5,586,307	183,751	1,739,919	536,518	1,709,676	1,787,567	11,543,738
TOTAL ...	27,859,624	863,133	8,339,202	2,400,467	9,514,778	8,424,920	57,402,124
Average ...	5,571,925	172,627	1,667,840	480,093	1,902,956	1,684,984	11,480,425
1886–87 ...	5,723,643	184,484	1,814,650	417,821	1,478,002	2,014,447	11,633,047
1887–88 ...	5,841,750	190,113	1,871,114	494,968	1,625,797	2,346,622	12,370,364
1888–89 ...	5,945,362	222,878	2,118,635	605,932	1,716,579	2,754,364	13,363,750
1889–90 ...	5,960,717	231,802	2,349,819	583,761	1,994,083	3,016,261	14,136,443
1890–91 ...	5,833,407	221,464	2,203,473	547,725	2,118,249	3,124,666	14,048,984
TOTAL ...	29,304,879	1,050,741	10,357,691	2,650,207	8,932,710	13,256,360	65,552,588
Average ...	5,860,976	210,148	2,071,538	530,042	1,786,542	2,651,272	13,110,518
1891–92 ...	5,516,461	242,671	2,165,631	760,117	2,155,734	3,295,463	14,136,077
1892–93 ...	6,068,078	212,673	2,399,055	744,223	1,906,352	2,989,893	14,320,274
1893–94 ...	6,505,739	230,195	2,373,796	569,372	1,748,992	2,910,283	14,338,377
1894–95 ...	6,158,803	231,910	2,635,726	530,201	1,000,504	2,931,050	13,488,194
1895–96 ...	6,332,482	222,492	2,096,777	616,154	2,089,743	3,797,357	15,155,005
TOTAL ...	30,581,563	1,139,941	11,670,985	3,220,067	8,901,325	15,924,046	71,437,927
Average ...	6,116,313	227,988	2,334,197	644,013	1,780,265	3,184,809 (*b*)	14,287,585
1896–97 ...	6,141,178	264,906	(*a*)	830,761	3,125,234	4,641,435 (*b*)	—
Demands.							
	Rs.	Rs.	Rs.	Rs.	Rs.	Rs.	Rs.
1891–92 ...	1,48,22,691	12,15,726	45,90,839	13,99,602	71,11,505	78,90,883	3,70,31,246
1892–93 ...	1,85,82,793	11,41,546	50,10,395	12,72,010	65,16,326	69,95,903	3,95,18,973
1893–94 ...	1,94,06,516	12,46,203	50,31,182	10,72,764	70,03,783	71,87,533	4,09,47,981
1894–95 ...	2,00,68,286	12,55,367	55,30,740	9,75,530	48,49,589	72,78,426	3,99,57,938
1895–96 ...	2,12,66,444	12,90,640	42,18,230	10,96,866	77,39,841	1,12,66,818	4,68,78,839
TOTAL ...	9,41,46,730	61,49,482	2,43,81,386	58,16,772	3,32,21,044	4,06,19,563	20,43,34,977
Average ...	1,88,29,346	12,29,896	48,76,277	11,63,354	66,44,209	81,23,913	4,08,66,995
1896–97 ...	1,95,73,083	12,54,634	(*a*)	15,34,398	1,08,46,722	1,42,12,490	—

(*a*) Return for Sind not received.

(*b*) The Punjab area figures include areas irrigated from the Native States Branches of the Sirhind and Western Jumna Canals.

N.B.—The figures in this statement include irrigation from (1) Major Works, (2) Minor Works for which capital accounts are kept, (3) Minor Works for which no capital accounts are kept.

Extract from the Proceedings of the Government of India, in the Department of Revenue and Agriculture—*No.* 36—240-5, *dated the* 30*th December* 1897.

READ—

Preliminary Narrative of the Famine in India in 1896–97 by T. W. Holderness, Esq., I.C.S., Deputy Secretary (Famine) to the Government of India.

Weather and Crop Reports for the various provinces published in the *Gazette of India*, dated the 1st January 1898.

RESOLUTION.

THE famine which since the close of 1896 has grievously afflicted so large a part of India, is now virtually at an end; and an abundant autumn harvest and conditions favourable to the spring crops have, throughout the greater part of the distressed tracts, once more put the people into good heart. The calamity, in respect of its intensity and of the area and population which it affected, though fortunately not in respect of its duration, has been more severe than any other famine of the century, and probably than any other which Indian history records. The tracts in which distress was acute or severe covered an aggregate area of 270,000 square miles with a population of 50,000,000, while distress of less intensity, but which still amounted to famine, prevailed over a further area of 33,000 square miles, with a population of 13,000,000. Thus the area throughout which relief operations were required was two-and-a-half times that of the United Kingdom, while the population for whose relief they were undertaken fell only just short of double the population of Great Britain. And there was probably no part of India in which the poorer classes did not suffer severely from the abnormally high prices which have obtained during the past year.

2. In coping with such a calamity the hands of the Government have been stronger than at any previous period. Since the last famine of comparable magnitude that afflicted the country—that of 1877–78—the irrigated area in which crops are reasonably secure and for which returns exist has increased by 17 per cent., and the area watered from large works constructed by the State from seven to ten million acres, while some five million acres are watered from smaller works under Government control. In 1877 less than 9,000 miles of railway were open. In 1897 the mileage exceeded 20,000; and nothing in the experience of the past year has been more striking than the freedom with which grain has passed from place to place in accordance with fluctuations of prices, and the manner in which the prices of food staples have maintained a general level throughout large tracts, in parts of which the harvests have been excellent. The scarcity prices which obtained over considerable areas during former famines have, except for a very short time, over very limited tracts, and under very exceptional circumstances, never even been approached on the present occasion; and while the improvement of communications has probably operated to make high prices more general than they otherwise would have been, it has certainly done much to diminish the intensity of distress where distress was most acute. The experience of the past year has shown that the reserve of food stocks in India is, even when preceding harvests have been unfavourable, larger than could have been foreseen; and the external help that has been afforded amounts to under 700,000 tons, of which 600,000 were rice from Burma. In parts of the country, however, the local reserves were exhausted at an early stage of the scarcity; and the Government of India believe that the readiness with which the demand thus arising was supplied from the resources of other and more favoured tracts, is due in no small measure to the policy of absolute abstention from interference with private enterprise, which, save in the case of very limited areas of which the circumstances were most exceptional, has been scrupulously observed throughout. Nor is it only in material respects that the position has been stronger now than formerly. The experience of previous famines has not been thrown away; and the approach of

scarcity found for the first time an organisation elaborated in readiness for the struggle, and the main principles on which it was to be conducted laid down beforehand. The Famine Codes of the various provinces have been subjected to the severest possible test; it has disclosed in them defects which will now be corrected; but on the whole they have borne the trial well.

3. In the relief of distress and the prevention of death from privation the Government of this country have incurred a direct expenditure of between seven and eight crores of rupees; they have distributed about two crores more in the shape of loans for the construction of wells, for the purchase of seed and bullocks, and for other agricultural purposes; and they have suspended over two crores of land revenue, of which a substantial portion will not be recovered. This public expenditure has been supplemented by private charity of the most splendid nature. Rs. 29,16,000 have been contributed to the Indian Famine Charitable Relief Fund by India itself, Rs. 1,22,51,000 by Great Britain, Rs. 11,23,000 by other British Colonies, of which more than half came from Canada, and Rs. 2,46,000 by Foreign countries, making, in addition to valuable gifts in kind, an aggregate of Rs. 1,65,36,000. The money has been expended in the relief of distress which refused from honourable motives to accept public aid, in supplying additional comforts to the aged, the infirm, and the diseased, in providing for children whom famine has deprived of their natural guardians, and (perhaps most important and most valuable of all) in giving a fresh start in life to those who had lost their means of livelihood in the struggle for existence. The good thus done has been incalculable, and has called forth the deepest gratitude from the inarticulate millions who have benefited by it. Nor do the public subscription lists by any means exhaust the tale of private liberality. Large sums of money have been sent from various parts of the world, especially to Missionary agencies, and have been applied to the relief of distress. In this connection the cargo of grain contributed by charitable persons in America and despatched at the expense of the Government of the United States deserves special mention. Gentlemen, both European and Native, who derive their wealth from the land, have expended large sums in assisting the cultivators of the estates in which they were interested; and throughont the country smaller people have exercised, according to their means, that private charity which so honourably distinguishes the people of India. In all, relief for one day has been given at the expense of Government to 834 million units. In operations of such magnitude, mistakes are inevitable. But the Government of India believe that they were seldom serious, either in their nature or in their extent, and that in all cases they were promptly detected and remedied.

4. No measures of relief, however perfect and extensive, can prevent privation and distress at a time such as the past year has been; and privation and distress, when continued for long months together, must of necessity affect the death-roll, if only by increasing the susceptibility and weakening the power of resistance to disease, and by hastening the decease of those whose natural term was in any case approaching its close. Some of the parts of India in which distress was most acute are inhabited by passive and timorous forest tribes, habitually suspicious of Government interference; some are traversed by the great highways along which enormous numbers of the poorer classes annually pass from province to province in search of that employment which the varying agricultural seasons afford; in some provinces the re-establishment of the normal rainfall has been accompanied or followed, as often in former famines, by a wave of malarial fever. But the Governor-General in Council believes that the task of preserving human life which has for nearly a twelvemonth taxed the energies and the resources of the administration of almost every province in India, has been performed with conspicuous success.

5. No mere expenditure of money, however lavish, could have secured that success, unless accompanied by untiring devotion to duty on the part of those charged with its administration. The functions of the Supreme Government have necessarily been confined to providing the necessary funds when provincial resources were exhausted, and to exercising the most general supervision over the broad principles upon which relief was administered. Upon the heads of the Provincial Governments and their advisers devolved the heavy responsibility of watching the pulse of local distress, of instantly adopting measures varied to

suit the varying conditions, and of holding an even balance between the claims of the unfortunate and the duty of public economy. The Governor General in Council desires to recognise most cordially the manner in which that responsibility has been discharged, and the high sense of duty which has animated those upon whom it fell. Upon the Divisional and District Officers, working in concert with the local officers of the Public Works, Medical, Police, Forest and other Departments, has lain the task of carrying into effect the scheme of relief, the success of which was mainly dependent upon their watchful and active care. It is these officers and their assistants, European and Native, Civil, Military and non-official, who have most literally borne the burden and heat of the day; and some indeed have sacrificed their own lives in the successful effort to save the lives of others. There are many also who hold no official position, who have laboured with assiduity and self-devotion to save life and relieve suffering. All have done their duty nobly under the most trying circumstances; and his Excellency in Council desires publicly to express his admiration of the manner in which their fight to save life has been conducted. It will be found that the customary means of rewarding merit have not been overlooked, but the number of those who can be thus individually distinguished is necessarily small. The knowledge that they have done their duty and have earned the gratitude of the poor and helpless will remain with all who have done good service in the struggle, and his Excellency in Council is anxious to add this recognition of their work, which he is sure that public opinion will emphatically and universally endorse.

6. Finally, the Governor General in Council desires to express his admiration of the manner in which the people of the country have endured the calamity. When prices rose at the first approach of scarcity, there were a few unimportant cases of local disturbance; and the amount of petty crime has no doubt been generally increased by the prevalence of famine. But as a whole, the inhabitants of the tracts affected have endured the suffering which no efforts either of public or of private charity could do more than mitigate, with a patience and a fortitude that are beyond all praise. The marvellous power of recuperation which the population of India possess has often been the subject of remark; and His Excellency in Council earnestly hopes that within the next few years, favourable seasons will have restored the people to prosperity, and have obliterated at any rate all material traces of what they suffered during the famine of 1897.

ORDER.—Ordered that copies of the above Resolution be forwarded to the Local Governments and Administrations noted in the margin * for information.

* Government of Madras.
,, Bombay.
,, Bengal.
,, N.-W. P. & Oudh.
,, Punjab.
,, Burma.
Chief Commissioner, Central Provinces.
Chief Commissioner, Assam.
,, Coorg.
,, Ajmere-Merwara.
Resident at Hyderabad.

Ordered also, that copies be forwarded to the Finance, Public Works, Home and Foreign Departments for information.

Ordered also, that a copy be published in the *Gazette of India* for general information.

[True extract.]

DENZIL IBBETSON,

Secretary to the Government of India